101

THINGS

YOU DIDN'T KNOW ABOUT

COLUMBUS

OHIO

(BUT ARE ABOUT TO FIND OUT)

BY
HORACE MARTIN WOODHOUSE

Dedication

To the John and Jane Smiths of Columbus

(It is said that each person to whom a book is
dedicated, always buys a copy. If it proves true in
this instance, good fortune is about to smile upon
THE AUTHOR.)

INTRODUCTION

*Awareness of the past is an important element
in the love of place.*
— Yi-Fu Tuan

According to James Thurber, Columbus-born author
and celebrated wit, "Columbus is a town in which almost
anything is likely to happen, and in which almost everything has." To prove Thurber's point, your curious author
has dug up bits of esoterica – odd, amusing, and little-
known strands that make up the city's variegated fabric.

Sure, you live here, but how much do you really know
about Columbus? Can you name your hometown football
heroes, *Playboy Magazine* playmates, Pop Movement lu-
minary, Pulitzer Prize-winning historian, World War I
flying ace, the local boxer who became heavyweight champion, or the local girl who became Miss America (twice!)?
Who was the Columbus-born general the troops called
"Old Iron Pants"? Or the local aviator who became the
first woman to fly solo around the world? How did a bor-
der dispute lead to the greatest rivalry in college football?
Where was the city's (and the world's) first service station?
What in the world was Abraham Lincoln's body doing
here? Readers learn the answers to these intriguing ques-
tions and much, much more.

Fascinating tangents and tidbits in purposely random
sequence (with generous cross-references) create a ready-
to-explore trail of knowledge about Columbus and its envi-
rons, informing and entertaining, correcting myths and
misconceptions, mostly revealing a quaint, curious, and un-
expected treasure trove that brings a culture and a place
into sharp focus.

1. The City That Almost Wasn't

A member of the territorial legislature, Thomas Worthington worked tirelessly for the admission of Ohio into the Union. He personally traveled to Washington, D.C. to urge President Thomas Jefferson to approve the Enabling Act of 1802 which called on the people of Ohio to form a constitutional convention. Ohio, its name derived from the Indian word for "beautiful river," became the seventeenth state of the United States in 1803, but had yet to designate a permanent capital.

Political maneuvering nearly landed the capital in Zanesville or Chillicothe, however, in 1810, the legislature appointed five commissioners to select a more central location, one that was equally accessible from all corners of the state. Included for consideration were Dublin, Franklinton, Delaware, and Worthington. The commissioners favored Franklinton, a small town laid out by surveyor Lucas Sullivant (see **Bottoms Up**, page 10), named in honor of Benjamin Franklin, on the west side of the Scioto River (the major transportation route at that time), however, they would not have the last word.

Four land speculators, John Kerr, James Johnson, Alexander McLaughlin, and Lyne Starling, had acquired a 1,200-acre tract of land opposite Franklinton. Although it was mostly uninhabited forest, the group offered to put up $50,000 to develop the capital at the site. The General Assembly accepted their offer on February 14, 1812, and at the suggestion of saloonkeeper Joseph Foos, the new city was named in honor of explorer Christopher Columbus.

2. Spizzerinctum

The son of a local jeweler, Maynard Edward "Jack" Sensenbrenner was born in Circleville, 25 miles outside of Columbus. He graduated from Circleville High School, then followed his sweetheart, Mildred Harriet Sexauer (the niece of a former mayor of Lancaster) to California where he supported himself as a Fuller Brush Man. Jack and Mildred married in 1927 and returned to Columbus, settling on the West Side where he opened a religious bookstore.

Although his political ads on TV were uncommon tactics at the time and dismissed as Madison Avenue gimmickery, in 1954 Sensenbrenner became the first Democratic mayor of Columbus in two decades. During his terms as mayor, he laid the groundwork for massive growth of Columbus by requiring all neighborhoods that accepted city water service to be annexed into the city. Under his leadership Columbus grew by more than 100 square miles.

An eccentric political character, his vocabulary included terms like spizzerinctum (meaning guts, backbone, chutzpah) which he said made "Columbus, the United States of America, the Boy Scouts of America ... absolutely dynamic." (He picked up the term from his high school football coach). His creed, "God, Love and Country," helped Columbus win the coveted "All America City" award in 1958.

3. "Buckeye Bullet"

The tenth child of Henry and Emma Alexander Owens, James Cleveland (called "J.C.") was born in Oakville, Alabama on September 12, 1913. At the age of nine, his family moved to Cleveland, where a schoolteacher unwittingly changed his name. As the teacher took names for the class roll, he responded, "J.C." She misunderstood his Southern accent and entered "Jesse" in the roll book. The name stuck, and he would be known as Jesse Owens for the rest of his life.

After attending Cleveland East Technical High School, where he tied the world record in the 100-yard dash as a senior, Owens attended Ohio State, but only after local employment was found for his father, ensuring the family could be supported. Affectionately known as the "Buckeye Bullet," he won a record eight individual NCAA championships, four each in 1935 and 1936. But he was never awarded a scholarship for his efforts, so he continued to work part-time jobs to pay for school.

In 1936, as Owens arrived in Berlin to compete for the United States in the Summer Olympics, he was persuaded by Adi Dassler, the founder of Adidas, to wear the company's shoes – the first-ever sponsorship for a male African-American athlete. During the games, Nazi propaganda promoted concepts of "Aryan racial superiority," depicting ethnic Africans as inferior. Owens rained on Adolph Hitler's parade by winning four gold medals.

4. Lincoln on His Way Home

President Abraham Lincoln was assassinated on Good Friday, April 14, 1865. After millions of citizens attended the funeral procession in Washington, D.C., his body was transported 1,700 miles through New York to Springfield, Illinois. Arrangements for the Lincoln funeral train were directed by Secretary of War Edwin M. Stanton who appointed Ohio Governor John Brough to head a "Committee of Arrangements" for the trip back to his hometown.

Lincoln's body began the journey on April 21. The funeral train, whose engine had the President's photograph hung over the cowcatcher, retraced the route he traveled as President-elect. To help preserve Lincoln's body during the 12 day trip, it was packed in ice.

On Saturday, April 29, the train arrived in Columbus at 7:30 AM. Lincoln's casket traveled south on High Street to Broad, east on Broad, then through several of the downtown neighborhood streets until coming back on Town Street to High Street. All along the way, thousands of mourners lined the streets, houses draped in black.

The procession arrived at the Statehouse, adorned in black crepe for the occasion, where the President laid in state in the rotunda. It was estimated that 8,000 people an hour walked past the casket. At 8 PM the train departed Columbus and headed for Indianapolis.

5. Seeds of Learning

The school was called the Ohio Agriculture and Mechanical College when twenty-four students met for classes at the old William Neil (see **Tycoon**, page 49) farm property on September 17, 1873. The state's General Assembly had established the new college through the provisions of the Land-Grant Act, signed by President Lincoln eleven years earlier. This legislation revolutionized the nation's approach to higher education, bringing a college degree within reach of all high school graduates.

The college's curriculum was a matter of bitter dispute among politicians, the public, and educators. Some hoped that the college would devote itself solely to the teaching of agriculture and mechanical arts, however, Governor Rutherford B. Hayes (see **Man Who Would Be President**, page 48) imagined more than a "cow college" and fought for a comprehensive program that featured English and ancient and foreign languages. Harvard educated professor of geology Edward Francis Baxter Orton Sr. was named the first president of Ohio A&M.

In 1878 the school's name was changed to Ohio State University. In that same year the first class of six men graduated, and in 1879, the university graduated its first women (see **Safe House**, page 51). By 1900, Ohio State had approximately one thousand students; by 2000, it was the nation's second largest institution of higher education with an enrollment of 47,000.

6. When Every Day Was Sunday

William Ashley "Billy" Sunday was one of the great American preachers of religion. The fiery evangelist conducted over 300 crusades in the 39 years of his ministry, preaching to over 100,000,000 people, the greatest number prior to Billy Graham.

His "fire and brimstone" sermons were incredibly popular. He traveled from town to town, holding revival meetings, condemning liquor, birth control, and other sins of the age. For 49 days, from late December 1912 carrying over into February 1913, Sunday preached in Goodale Park (see **House Calls in Columbus**, page 96), one of his longest crusades, netting donations totaling $21,000.

In a huge tabernacle-tent with sawdust covering the ground, every chair was filled twice daily and three times on Sundays. He would berate his audience, telling them that they were doomed to Hell if they did not immediately give up their sinful ways and dedicate themselves to God's word as printed in the Bible. After he preached his celebrated booze sermon on the afternoon of Sunday, January 26, at least one local saloonkeeper became converted and quit the business.

It is estimated that up to ten percent of the people in Columbus, roughly 18,000 people, "walked the sawdust trail" to receive Jesus Christ as Savior.

7. Boy in Ohio

Philip David Ochs was born in El Paso, Texas, on December 19, 1940, to Jacob "Jack" Ochs, a doctor, and Gertrude Phin Ochs. The family moved frequently, to Far Rockaway, New York, when Phil was a teenager, to Perrysburg in upstate New York, where he first studied music, and then to Columbus. From 1956 to 1958, he was a student at the Staunton Military Academy in rural Virginia; upon graduation he returned to Columbus and enrolled at Ohio State to study journalism.

It was at OSU where Ochs developed an interest in politics, particularly fascinated with the Cuban Revolution, and where he met Jim Glover, a fellow student and folk musician. Glover taught him to play the guitar and introduced him to the music of Pete Seeger, Woody Guthrie, and The Weavers.

Ochs arrived in New York City in 1962 and began performing politically-influenced songs in small folk nightclubs, eventually becoming an integral part of the Greenwich Village folk music scene. During the early period of his career, Ochs and Bob Dylan had a friendly rivalry. Dylan said of Ochs, "You're not a folksinger. You're a journalist." Ochs became involved in the creation of the Youth International Party, known as the Yippies, along with Jerry Rubin and Abbie Hoffman.

Ochs' boyhood in Columbus provided the inspiration for his song "Boy in Ohio."

8. Mass Production

By 1882, the Columbus Buggy Company, founded by Clinton Dewitt Firestone, was the largest horse-drawn buggy manufacturer on earth, turning out a finished product "every eight minutes during a ten-hour work day," pioneering what became known as "mass production" and building buggies priced within the reach of the average family. Its plant covered an entire city block, and by 1900, the company employed over 1000 local workers.

Both Harvey S. Firestone (Clinton's cousin) and Eddie Rickenbacker (see **Fast Eddie**, page 71) got their early business experience while working at the Columbus Buggy Company, before moving on to other ventures. Harvey went on to the tire business in the 1890s and shared some of the innovative methods his Columbus relative had developed with automaker Henry Ford

With the advent of the automobile, buggy and carriage manufacturers faced serious competition. Like some other companies, the Columbus Buggy Company's management decided to begin producing powered buggies, using both electric and gasoline engines. Unfortunately, these changes were not enough for the company to survive, as auto manufacturers were already being drawn to the port city of Detroit where raw materials could be brought in by ship. The Columbus Buggy Company went bankrupt in 1913.

9. Strokes of Genius

Born in Columbus on August 12, 1882, George Wesley Bellows attended Ohio State from 1901 to 1904, where he provided illustrations for *The Makio*, the student yearbook. He left the university just before he was to graduate and moved to New York City to study art with Robert Henri at the New York School of Art. He became associated with Henri's "The Eight" and the Ashcan School, a group of artists who advocated painting contemporary American society in all its forms. By 1906, Bellows was renting his own studio.

His urban New York scenes depicted the chaos of working-class people, and a series of paintings portraying amateur boxing matches became his signature contribution to art history. These paintings are characterized by dark atmospheres, through which the bright, roughly lain brushstrokes of the human figures vividly strike with a strong sense of motion and direction. Bellows became the most acclaimed American artist of his generation.

In addition to painting, Bellows made significant contributions to lithography, helping to expand the use of the medium as a fine art. He also illustrated numerous books in his later career, including several by H.G. Wells.

The Columbus Museum of Art has a sizeable collection of both his portraits and New York street scenes. In December 1999, "Polo Crowd," a 1910 Bellows painting, sold for $27.5 million to Microsoft founder Bill Gates.

10. Bottoms Up

At the conclusion of the Revolutionary War, Virginia and other states were asked to cede their western land claims to the government in order to develop the Northwest and Southwest Territories. In 1784, Virginia relinquished its claim to lands to the northwest of the Ohio River in exchange for the right to award bounty lands (land grants in lieu of payment for military service) in Ohio's "Virginia Military District." The United States Congress ordered surveys and subdivision of the land.

It was a surveyor by the name of Lucas Sullivant (born in September of 1765 in Mecklenburgh County, Virginia) who, in 1797, laid out a town on the western bank of the Scioto River, near the place where the Scioto and Whetstone Creek, now the Olentangy River (see **Misnomer**, page 13), came together. Sullivant named the town "Franklinton" because he was an admirer of Benjamin Franklin.

While the fertile, low-lying land was ideal for farming in the early days, much of the area lies below the level of the rivers. Severe flooding events in the Franklinton area have occurred, first in 1798, only a year after the town was settled, and again in 1898, 1913 (93 fatalities) and 1959. A seven-and-a-quarter-mile floodwall designed by the Army Corps of Engineers now protects "The Bottoms."

11. House of the Future

At the end of World War II, the American G.I. came home to marry the girl he'd left behind, buy a home, and start a family. But housing construction had virtually stopped during the war years, compounding a critical shortage in residential housing.

In 1947, Chicago industrialist and inventor Carl Strandlund, who had previously designed prefabricated gas stations, obtained a $12.5 million Reconstruction Finance Corporation loan to mass produce pre-fab, porcelain-enameled steel houses with steel framing and steel interior walls and ceiling. His "Lustron House" promised to do for housing what Henry Ford had done for the Model T – make an "Everyman" house. From its plant in Columbus (the rented Curtiss-Wright airframe factory), Strandlund's firm constructed 2,560 houses between 1948 and 1950, each selling for between $8,500 and $9,500 – about 25 percent less than comparable conventional housing.

Lustron Houses faced strong opposition from labor unions, who saw mass production as a direct threat to workers in the construction industry. Some accounts suggest an organized effort from the existing housing industry to stop Strandlund. Lustron declared bankruptcy in 1950, despite a well-publicized, government-supported enterprise, manufacturing a desperately-needed product.

12. Raising Lazarus

The first Jewish families began settling in Columbus in 1840, emigrating from Bavaria and Prussia, where anti-Semitism had begun to take root in parallel with the growth of German nationalism. In 1850, an entrepreneurial Jewish immigrant by the name of Simon Lazarus opened a one-room men's clothing store on South High Street with $3,000 capital and a single employee.

By 1870, with improvements to the garment industry brought about by the demand for Civil War uniforms, Simon's store expanded to include ready-made men's civilian clothing and eventually a complete line of merchandise. After Simon's death in 1877, his sons, Fred and Ralph took over the store, adding a women's and children's department. In 1909, Fred's son supervised the construction of a new five-story structure which included a live alligator on display, a tearoom, an auditorium for exhibits and meetings, and a permanent home in Columbus for Santa Claus.

Lazarus installed the first department store escalators in the country. Air conditioning was added to the selling floors in 1934, making it one of the first big stores in America to promise shoppers a "cool" experience. Lazarus was influential in the American retail industry for over 150 years, particularly during the early 20th century as a founding partner in Federated Department Stores, and continued until the nameplate was retired on March 6, 2005, in favor of Macy's.

13. Misnomer

The Olentangy River flows 88 miles from its headwaters in Crawford and Richland Counties through Marion and Morow counties into Delaware and ending in Franklin County at the confluence with the Scioto River in downtown Columbus.

Long before early settlers made their way to what is now Ohio, Deleware Indians had named the river Keenhongsheconsepung, meaning "stone for your knife stream." The abundant concentrations of shale along its shores were ideal for sharpening knives and other tools. Since the Indian name was unpronounceable to the white settlers, they called it "Whetstone Creek."

In 1833, well-meaning state legislators began an effort to restore Indian names to the state's waterways, and Whetstone Creek was mistakenly called the "Olentangy River." The word "Olentangy" literally means "river of red face paint," a name that actually belonged to Big Darby Creek further to the west, where local Wyandotte Indians obtained red clay for their face paint (the color red applied in preparation for battle). The Olentangy River should properly have been named the Whetstone River after its largest tributary. Oops!

In 1843 the United States government sent the remaining Wyandottes off to a reservation in Kansas. They were the last Indian Nation to leave Ohio.

14. Stay the Course

Born in Urbana, Ohio, on December 29, 1925, Paul B. "Pete" Dye was a golf-obsessed salesman for the Connecticut Mutual Life Insurance Company. After visiting Scotland to study the legendary courses, he made a gradual career transition into golf course design. His first well-known course was Crooked Stick Golf Club in Carmel, Indiana, opened in 1964.

Three years later he was tapped by Fred Jones for a project in the Columbus suburb of New Albany, simply called The Golf Course. Jones instructed Dye to build a course that would "feel as if it's been here forever as soon as it's finished." The fledgling architect kept true to the farmland heritage of the property with tree-lined corridors, generous fairways, and waving fields of native grasses.

Dye used a twenty-seven year old Columbus native by the name of Jack Nicklaus (see **The Golden Bear**, page 58), to consult on the integrity and "playability" of the course throughout the design process. The two men later teamed up at Harbour Town Golf Links, the course that catapulted Dye into prominence and started Nicklaus' prolific player-architect career.

After a long and distinguished career, Pete Dye's golf courses are among the most exciting in the world and are known best for their level of difficulty and extraordinary beauty.

15. The Lindbergh Line

After his historic non-stop flight from New York to Paris, Charles Lindbergh joined the fledgling commercial air carrier Transcontinental Air Transport Company (TAT), formed by the merging of Pennsylvania Railroad with the Atchison, Topeka and Sante Fe Railroads. TAT planned to combine trains and planes to efficiently transport passengers coast-to-coast, and they put Columbus on the route. After a local bond levy failed in 1927, Lindbergh visited Columbus to promote an $850,000 construction bond. The bond eventually passed on November 6, 1928, and Lindbergh selected the site for Port Columbus.

On July 7, 1929, TAT inaugurated service on the route laid out by Lindbergh from New York to Los Angeles via Columbus, affectionately called "The Lindbergh Line." Port Columbus became the eastern transfer point for TAT passengers traveling cross-country by rail and air. Nineteen daring people including famed aviatrix Amelia Earhart, who promoted aviation to women travelers for TAT, made the first westbound trip.

After less than two years, the scheduled train-plane operation was suspended after introduction of all-air coast-to-coast service by the renamed and merged company of Transcontinental and Western Air (TWA). By 1939, 15 flights operated by both TWA and American Airlines were taking off from Port Columbus every day.

16. Fill 'Er Up!

The Standard Oil Company of Ohio, organized in the form of a monopolistic trust by John D. Rockefeller, established a strong foothold in the U.S. and other countries in the transportation, production, refining, and marketing of petroleum products.

After the government forced a breakup of the Standard Oil Trust in 1911, two company executives, B.A. Mathews and H.S. Hollingsworth, recognized that gasoline-driven automobiles were the wave of the future. To take advantage of this opportunity, the two men created America's first ever service station in Columbus.

The business began operation on June 1, 1912, with a portable drive-thru located at the corner of Oak and Young Streets. Customers entered from the front, had their tanks filled by hand-cranked pumps with Standard "Red Crown" gasoline. It was called a "filling station," a name that would endure, even as late as the 1970s. The 14 x 20-foot building was managed by Harvey Wickliffe, a tank wagon driver for Standard Oil.

The station operated without electricity in the early days, so service ended at sundown. At times there were dozens of cars waiting in line, a success that prompted other oil companies to open their own filling stations throughout the city, state, and across the nation.

17. Muck Fichigan!

Every year during the final gridiron contest of the Big Ten Conference, between Ohio and Michigan, tensions run high. Ohio State coach Woody Hayes (see **Refuse to Lose,** page 44), famous for his hatred of Michigan, called it "that state up north" or "that team up north." He couldn't even bring himself to say the name. But the rivalry didn't begin with college football. It began in 1835 when Michigan claimed a 468-square-mile area that had been surveyed by Ohio at the beginning of its statehood. Militias were mobilized and sent to positions on opposite sides of the Maumee River near Toledo, but besides mutual taunting, there was little interaction between the two forces.

When Michigan sought statehood, it wanted to include the disputed territory within its boundaries, but Ohio's Congressional delegation was able to halt Michigan's admission to the Union until they gave up their claim.

It was during this dispute that Ohioans branded Michiganders as "wolverines," the insatiable gluttons of the weasel family whose pungent odor has given rise to the nicknames "skunk bear" and "nasty cat." Years later, the University of Michigan unwittingly adopted the wolverine as its school mascot.

"Carmen Ohio," the hymn-like OSU alma mater (see **Song of Ohio**, page 55) was likely written on the team's ride home to Columbus following a 1902 contest, in which Ohio State lost to Michigan 86-0.

18. Almost Disneyland

The first amusement park in Columbus was called "The Villa." Opened in 1880 by Robert M. Turner, the park consisted of picnic grounds, swimming pool, and a tavern. Three years later, the Columbus Street and Railroad Company realized the potential of increased ridership to a venue at the end of the line. They purchased the property and renamed it Olentangy Park.

In 1899, the local Dussenbury brothers purchased the park, built a theater and dance pavilion, and installed a carousel and rides such as the loop-the-loop, whirlwind, and shoot-the-chutes. Experiencing financial difficulty, in 1923 the Dussenbury brothers sold the park to a group called the Olentangy Amusement Company, managed by one Mr. Max Stern who introduced a roller coaster, Ferris wheel, tunnel of love, and many more attractions.

In 1929, new owners Leo and Elmer Haenlein added an outdoor ballroom and operated the park until 1938 when it was shut down to make room for the Olentangy Village apartment complex, developed by Leslie. L. LeVeque (see **Towering Achievement**, page 59). In 1940, LeVeque constructed Olentangy Lanes, a mammoth bowling alley on the site of the Park's former parking lot. It would stand until destroyed by fire in 1980.

In the 1970s, there were rumors that the Walt Disney Company had their eye on the former Olentangy Park property as the site for a Disney World in Columbus.

19. Reality Check

Born on March 1, 1837 in Martin's Ferry, Ohio, William Dean Howells was the second of William Cooper and Mary Dean Howells' eight children. His father was a newspaper editor and printer, and most of the boy's education came from reading at home and working at his father's print shop.

At the age of 19, in 1856, Howells moved to Columbus, where he worked as a reporter and city editor for *The Ohio State Journal* (the Republican Party's main voice in central Ohio). Involvement in Republican Party politics led members to commission him to write campaign literature for presidential candidate Abraham Lincoln. That work paid enough for Howells to travel to New England and meet, among others, Nathaniel Hawthorne, Ralph Waldo Emerson, Henry David Thoreau, and Walt Whitman. Returning to Columbus, he met Elinor Mead, a young woman who was visiting her cousin, Rutherford B. Hayes (see **Man Who Would Be President**, page 48). They were married in 1862.

With his effective use of native backgrounds, manners, and speech, Howells is regarded as "the father of American Realism." His style broke new ground, influencing such writers as Mark Twain (who he met on Twain's visit to Columbus for a public lecture on January 5, 1872). Howells remained proud of his Ohio roots throughout his life, returning to Columbus for the Ohio Centennial Celebration in 1888.

20. The Thrush from Columbus

Born in Chillicothe, Ohio, on February 20, 1937, Nancy Wilson was the first of six children born to Olden Wilson (iron foundry worker) and Lillian Ryan (domestic worker). She grew up listening to Dinah Washington, Ruth Brown, LaVerne Baker, and Little Esther Phillips. By the age of four, she knew she wanted to follow in their footsteps.

At the age of 15, while a student at West High School in Columbus, she won a talent contest sponsored by local television station WTVN. The prize was an appearance on a twice-a-week television show, *Skyline Melodies*, which she ended up hosting. In 1956, she auditioned and won a spot with Rusty Bryant's Carolyn Club Big Band; she toured with them throughout Canada and the Midwest from 1956 to 1958.

It was Julian "Cannonball" Adderley who suggested that she move to New York, where she was signed by Capitol Records in 1960. Nancy's debut single, "Guess Who I Saw Today," was so successful that between April 1960 and July 1962, Capitol released five Nancy Wilson albums. Over the years her repertoire has included pop style ballads, jazz and blues, show tunes, and standards. She has recorded over 60 albums, half of which have appeared on the Billboard charts; from 1963 to 1971 she logged eleven songs on the Hot 100.

Her colleague and long time friend Joe Williams called her "the thrush from Columbus."

21. Bush with Many Branches

The Grandfather of President George H. W. Bush and Great-Grandfather of George W. Bush, Samuel Prescott Bush, was born in Orange, New Jersey, on October 4, 1863, the son of Harriet Fay and the Rev. James Smith Bush, an Episcopal minister at Grace Church in Orange. He grew up in New Jersey, but spent the majority of his adult life in Columbus.

Bush graduated from Stevens Institute of Technology in Hoboken in 1884, where he played on one of the earliest college football teams. He became a mechanic's apprentice with the Pittsburgh, Cincinnati, Chicago and St. Louis Railroad in Logansport, Indiana, later transferring to Columbus, where in 1891 he became Master Mechanic. In 1901, he became General Manager of Buckeye Steel Castings, a manufacturer of railway parts run by Frank Rockefeller, the brother of oil magnate John D. Rockefeller. In 1908, Rockefeller retired and Bush became President of Buckeye, a position he would hold until 1927, becoming one of the top industrialists of his generation. Bush was the first president of the Ohio Manufacturers Association and co-founder of Scioto Country Club and Columbus Academy.

His son, Prescott Sheldon Bush, born in Columbus on May 15, 1895, attended Yale, became a Wall Street executive banker, and a United States Senator representing Connecticut from 1952 until January 1963.

22. You *Can* Go Home Again

James Grove Thurber was born in Columbus on December 8, 1894, to Charles Leander and Mary Agnes Thurber. He attended local public schools and graduated high school with honors in 1913, then went on to attend Ohio State from 1913 to 1917.

Thurber launched his professional writing career as a reporter for the *Columbus Dispatch* (see **Breaking News**, page 66) in 1920. He moved to New York City in 1926 and began writing for the New Yorker after friend E.B. White (*Charlotte's Web*) got him a job at the magazine. In collaboration with White he produced his first book, *Is Sex Necessary?* By 1931, the first of his absurdist cartoons began appearing in the *New Yorker*.

Thurber's writings mixed comical reminiscences of his childhood with wry observations on modern times and the battle of the sexes. His best-known short story is *The Secret Life of Walter Mitty*, the tale of a mild-mannered man who escapes into heroic daydreams. But Columbus was never out of Thurber's thought or out of his writing. All the stories in his masterpiece of American humor, *My Life and Hard Times*, are set in Columbus.

Thomas Wolfe suggested "You can't go home again," but after Thurber's death on November 2, 1961, his cremated remains were returned to Columbus and buried in Green Lawn Cemetery (see **Final Resting Place**, page 24) near his parents and maternal grandparents.

23. Ripe for the Picking

Alexander W. Livingston was born in Reynoldsburg, Ohio, on October 14, 1821, the son of John and Mary Graham Livingston, who had moved to Ohio from Cambridge, New York. At the age of twenty-one, Livingston began working for a local seed grower. In 1852, he purchased seventy acres of land and began exploring ways to develop new and improved vegetables for what became the A.W. Livingston Buckeye Seed Gardens of Columbus.

In particular, he was obsessed with the original wild tomato, a sour-tasting, cherry-sized berry with ruffles and ridges. Livingston spent years on a quest to develop a commercial tomato with a smooth contour, larger uniform size and better flavor. After many attempts at hybridization, he began a process of selecting seeds from tomato plants that exhibited specific characteristics.

In 1870, Livingston introduced what is regarded to be the first-ever, perfectly uniform, smooth-skinned, deep scarlet-red tomato. No one had seen a tomato quite like it before. He called the new variety "Paragon," the first of some thirty-one tomato varieties that Livingston and his descendents introduced to the public between 1870 and 1941.

Reynoldsburg is recognized as "The Birthplace of the Tomato" and the "Tomato Festival" has been held every year since 1964. Thanks to Alexander Livingston, each man, woman and child in America now consumes almost 80 pounds of tomatoes every year.

24. Final Resting Place

The most fashionable and sought after "final address" in Columbus, Green Lawn Cemetery, founded in 1848, covers over 360 acres, incorporates over 25 miles of roads, paths, and lanes, and contains nearly 150,000 interments.

The crypts span the breadth of late-Victorian and turn-of-the-century architectural movements, including some styled in the Mesopotamian-Egyptian style, popularized by Howard Carter's discovery of King Tut's tomb in 1922. Some of the largest family crypts that can be seen are those of the Hayden, Battelle, and Packard families. Entombed in private burial plots surrounding the central crypt is the Lazarus family (see **Raising Lazarus**, page 12).

There is a special burial area called "Lullabye Land," where stillborns and infant deaths are laid to rest. Six distinct areas for war veterans, each dedicated to a specific American war, include the oldest section towards the western rear of the cemetery for Civil War veterans of Ohio infantry battalions. A famous monument is erected towards the westernmost boundary for the "Soldiers and Sailors" memorial movement.

Nearby, but unaffiliated, Green Lawn Abbey is a structure built in 1927 by the Columbus Mausoleum Company. Granite walls, marble fireplaces, stained glass windows, and religious statues adorn the final resting place of notable local figures, including magician Howard Thurston (see **The King of Cards**, page 62).

25. Knockout

Born in Columbus on April 7, 1960, James "Buster" Douglas, the son of professional boxer William "Dynamite" Douglas, attended Linden McKinley High School where he played football and basketball, leading Linden to a Class AAA state basketball championship in 1977.

He began a professional boxing career in 1981, and among his notable early fights were wins over Randall "Tex" Cobb and former WBA titleholder Greg Page. A knockout of Michael "Mercury" Williams on the undercard of Mike Tyson vs. Michael Spinks earned him a shot at the heavyweight championship.

On February 11, 1990, Douglas pulled off one of the most shocking upsets in boxing history when he knocked out undefeated champion Mike Tyson. At the time, Tyson was considered to be the best boxer in the world and one of the most feared heavyweight champions of all time. Later that year, he made his only defense of the title against Evander Holyfield. Douglas was knocked out in the third round and decided to retire after the fight, finishing his career with a record of 38-6-1.

Buster Douglas is one of the few non-students to be honored by Ohio State with the opportunity to dot the "I" (see **Dotting the "I,"** page 75) during the performance of the Script Ohio by the Ohio State Marching Band.

26. Humor in the Heartland

A TV sitcom set in Columbus, *Family Ties* aired on NBC for seven seasons, from 1982 to 1989. The show reflected the country's shift from the cultural liberalism of the 1960s to Reagan-era conservatism. President Reagan, in fact, called it his favorite show and reportedly offered to appear in an episode.

Family Ties was modeled after producer Gary David Goldberg and wife Diane's real-life experiences as former hippies transforming into suburban family life. The show's characters Elyse and Steven Keaton (Meredith Baxter and Michael Gross) were Baby Boomers and liberal Democrats, raising their three children, Alex (Michael J. Fox), Mallory (Justine Bateman), and Jennifer (Tina Yothers).

Michael J. Fox became a pop-culture role model for the political right as Alex P. Keaton, a briefcase-wielding teenage Republican. In the show's very first scene, Elyse and Steven subject the family to a slide show of their march on Washington, before the kids were born. The Keaton children mock their parents. "What were you protesting," Alex asks, "good grooming?" The show ended in 1989 after Alex leaves home for the first time, moving to a career on Wall Street.

The program won multiple awards, including three consecutive Emmy Awards for "Outstanding Lead Actor in a Comedy Series" by Michael J. Fox.

27. Wolfe Pack

Sons of Andrew Jackson Wolfe, a Civil War veteran and Ohio shoemaker, Robert Frederick Wolfe and Harry Preston Wolfe arrived in Columbus in 1888, established the Wolfe Brothers Shoe Company, and earned a fortune manufacturing low-priced shoes ("Wolfe Wear U Well"), at one time sold in 4,000 stores in 38 States.

The brothers were determined to dominate Columbus journalism as well as business life, and after purchasing *The Ohio State Journal* ("Columbus' 'Good Morning' Newspaper"), they acquired *The Columbus Dispatch* (see **Breaking News**, page 66).

Robert was the hell-raising, hotheaded partner (he once served time in prison for shooting a man who insulted a lady he was escorting). Quiet and shy, Harry Wolfe was the polar opposite. Together they became heavily involved in Republican politics, making "The Wigwam," the family's country estate southeast of Columbus, unofficial headquarters for party leaders.

The Wolfes and their families gathered at the secluded, wooded retreat, dotted with rustic lodges, a reception hall, movie theatre, and swimming pool, for parties that sometimes included several hundred guests, among them Warren Harding, Calvin Coolidge, Herbert Hoover, and Alf Landon.

The partnership ended suddenly in 1927, when Robert died in a suspicious fall from a fifth-floor window of the Dispatch building.

28. Where's the Beef?

According to *The Wall Street Journal*, Columbus is the "Fast Food Capital of the World." Fast food and mid-priced chains based here include Charley's Grilled Subs, Steak Escape, White Castle, Bob Evans Restaurants (see **The Case for Sausage**, page 83), Max & Erma's, Damon's Grill, Donatos Pizza and, of course, Wendy's.

David Thomas (see **Dave**, page 86) opened his first Wendy's Old Fashioned Hamburgers in downtown Columbus in November, 1969, offering fresh, made-to-order 100% domestic ground beef burgers, shaped in a square. He named the restaurant after his eight-year-old daughter Melinda Lou, who, when unable to say her own name at a very young age, called herself "Wendy."

Within a year, Thomas opened a second restaurant in Columbus, featuring what Wendy's calls "the first modern-day, drive-thru window," a formula for drive-thru operations that became a staple in the fast food industry. Wendy's first franchisee signed up in 1972 in Indianapolis. By 1976 there were 500 restaurants. The salad bar, another milestone for a national chain, was added in 1979. Today Wendy's operates in 34 countries with over 5,000 units in the US.

Columbus is the single largest per-capita restaurant-hosting town in America. Nearly every chain has at least one location here for testing and demographic purposes.

29. Family Tree

The use of the nickname "Buckeyes" for Ohio State athletic teams derives from the even wider use of the term in reference to all residents of the state of Ohio – thanks to William Henry Harrison.

The Buckeye, named for its large brown nuts, is a tree of the horse chestnut family, native throughout the Midwest, but not usually found further east. When white settlers arrived, they used these trees extensively for building log cabins.

In his run for President, William Henry Harrison of North Bend, Ohio, needed to trade his aristocratic background for a more populist image. His campaign manager, Horace Greeley, adopted the native buckeye tree and log cabins as campaign symbols. Harrison delegates carried buckeye canes, decorated with strings of buckeye beads. The campaign was notable because it marked the beginning of modern political campaigns based more on image than substance. The buckeye became indelibly linked with Ohio.

Harrison was elected President on March 4, 1841, but during his one hour and forty minute inaugural address he caught a terrible cold. President Harrison died April 4, 1841, after serving only one month in office.

OSU's Athletic Council officially adopted the term in 1950, but it had been in common use for many years before. Buckeye leaf decals are awarded to football players for outstanding efforts on the field.

30. Stone That Built Columbus

Limestone is a very strong rock, important for masonry and architecture, vying with only granite and sandstone as the most commonly used architectural stone. Many landmarks across the world, including the Great Pyramid in Giza, Egypt, are made of limestone.

The Marble Cliff Quarry in Columbus was at one time the largest limestone quarry in America, producing a variety of crushed limestone products that were used in the agriculture, construction and steel industries. The Kaufman family of Columbus owned and operated the 2,000-acre quarry property, stretching all the way from the Scioto River to the Olentangy River.

Such famous local landmarks as Ohio Stadium (see **Monument to College Football**, page 35), the Ohio Statehouse, the LeVeque Tower (see **Towering Achievement**, page 59), state and county airports and modern freeways were constructed from stone extracted from the quarry. Although the quarry was sold in the 1980s to investors who later developed the land into tracts of residential and commercial property, the northern section of the quarry is still mined today.

A notable structure in the village of Marble Cliff, built with stone from the nearby quarry, is the Bush Mansion, once the residence of local industrialist and entrepreneur Samuel Prescott Bush (see **Bush With Many Branches**, page 21), grandfather and great-grandfather of Presidents George H. W. Bush and George W. Bush.

31. The Real McCoys

Born in Steubenville, Ohio, on September 26, 1913, Dorothy Sloop Heflick performed under the stage name "Sloopy" in an all-female jazz band in New Orleans, from the 1930s through the 1950s. In 1963, songwriters Wes Farrell ("Boys") and Bert Russell ("Twist and Shout") collaborated on a song they claimed was inspired by Dorothy. Originally recorded by the Vibrations in 1964 as "My Girl Sloopy," the song climbed to #26 on the pop singles chart.

One year later, the McCoys, a group based in Dayton, Ohio, led by guitarist Rick Derringer, recorded a version called "Hang on Sloopy" that reached the #1 spot.

Dr. Charles Spohn, director of the OSU Marching Band, favored current music for halftime shows, and he regularly requested play lists from local radio stations. At Spohn's urging, arranger John Tagenhorst created a brass, instrumental arrangement of "Hang on Sloopy." First performed at the Ohio State-Illinois football game on October 9, 1965, the song became a lasting tradition.

In 1985, the General Assembly of Ohio formally named "Hang on Sloopy" as "The Official Rock Song of the State of Ohio." According to the RIAA.Recording Industry Association of America, "Hang on Sloopy" is one of the most performed songs in the history of music.

Dorothy Sloop Heflick retired to Florida and became a teacher. She died on July 28, 1998.

32. Infantry School

With the outbreak of the Civil War and the bombardment of Fort Sumter in South Carolina, President Abraham Lincoln asked Colonel Henry Beebe Carrington to raise troops for the expanded United States Army, and on July 10, 1861, he established a training camp on the Columbus farm of Solomon Beers at High Street south of its intersection with what is now Hudson Street. He named the new facility "Camp Thomas" in honor of Colonel Lorenzo Thomas, the Adjutant General of the U. S. Army, augmenting nearby Camp Chase (see **Northern Hospitality**, page 53).

For most of the war, Camp Thomas served as the headquarters for the 18th U.S. Infantry, a unit that made soldiers out of fugitives from the law, vagrants, and immigrants, mostly German and Irish. The camp remained active throughout the war, and served as a training base for fresh recruits needed to refill the ranks after the Battle of Stones River. Of the major battles of the Civil War, Stones River had the highest percentage of casualties on both sides.

By order of the Secretary of War, Camp Thomas was discontinued as a recruiting depot for the Regular Army early in October 1866. Barracks were sold, with some converted to houses in the vicinity of the camp.

At the end of the Civil War, the 18th Infantry was reassigned to protect the Bozeman Trail, an overland route connecting the gold rush territory of Montana to the Oregon Trail.

33. Smoke Gets in Your Eyes

In 1861, David Swisher of Newark, Ohio, acquired a small cigar business in settlement of a financial debt. Two of Swisher's four sons, John and Harry purchased the cigar business from their father in 1888, christening their business Swisher Brothers, and relocating to Columbus.

The two brothers quickly made their presence felt, taking what had been a one-room operation capable of making a few hundred cigars each day and turning it into one of Ohio's fastest growing businesses. By 1895, three local factories employed more than 1,000 workers who hand-rolled as many as 300,000 cigars each day.

The partnership ended in 1913 when John purchased Harry's interest in the company. and brought in his son Carl. The Swisher "King Edward Cigar" which had debuted in 1918 as a ten-cent cigar, sold for five cents following the introduction of rolling machines and was down to two cigars for a nickel by the end of the 1930s.

In 1923, John and Carl established corporate headquarters in Jacksonville, Florida, a community close to tobacco fields and shipping facilities. Four years later, the company's nearly 70-year presence in Columbus had come to an end. Facilities were closed and all production was consolidated into the company's Florida operations.

Today, Swisher International is a leader in the tobacco business, accounting for one-third of domestic cigar sales and is America's largest cigar exporter.

34. Unlimited Possibilities

In 1912, Bella Cabakoff emigrated with her parents from Russia and settled in Columbus. At age 21 she became the youngest buyer for the Lazarus Department Store (see **Raising Lazarus**, page 12).

In 1951, after spending over 20 years with Lazarus, she and her husband Harry Wexner opened a women's clothing store named Leslie's (after their son) on State Street. This store became the training ground for Leslie Wexner. In 1963, he borrowed $5,000 from his aunt and opened a store at the Kingsdale Shopping Center in Upper Arlington. His store was named "The Limited" because the merchandise was limited to clothing for young women, unlike his parents' general merchandise store. In 1964, Bella and Harry closed their store to join their son in his venture.

In 1969, Wexner took Limited Brands public, listed as LTD on the NYSE. The Company has since grown to over 2,800 stores and five major specialty retail brands. Included are Limited Stores, Express, Lerner New York, Lane Bryant and Structure. The Limited also owns approximately 84% of Intimate Brands, Inc., the leading specialty retailer of intimate apparel, beauty and personal care products through the Victoria's Secret, Bath & Body Works, and White Barn Candle Company brands.

35. Monument to College Football

Dwight Howard Smith (see **Ellen Griswold**, page 88) was born on February 21, 1886, in Dayton. In 1907, he graduated from Ohio State with a degree in Civil Engineering. After receiving a degree in Architecture at Columbia University, in 1918 he "came home" to Columbus, commissioned to design Ohio Stadium.

Nestled on the banks of the Olentangy River (see **Misnomer**, page 13), stately Ohio Stadium, better known as "The Horseshoe" or simply "The Shoe," has been home to the Buckeyes since October 7, 1922, when Ohio State played Ohio Wesleyan before a crowd of 20,000.

Prior to the construction of Ohio Stadium, the Buckeyes played their games at Ohio Field. The demand for a new stadium came about during the "Harley Years" (1916 to 1919), when Charles "Chic" Harley (see **The House That Harley Built**, page 73) became the Buckeyes' first three-time All-American. The stadium was funded entirely by fan donations and several stadium drives around the city where Harley would often appear.

One of the earliest stadiums constructed of concrete, many people feared that the structure would collapse. Originally, there were no restrooms for women, as it was considered unfashionable for women to attend sporting events, especially football games, during the 1920s.

With a seating capacity of 102,329, Ohio Stadium is the fourth largest on-campus facility in the nation.

36. Pen Pals

The Ohio Penitentiary was constructed in Columbus in 1834 and housed prisoners until 1979. Nationwide Arena now stands on the site of the abandoned "Old Pen."

Originally, the prison system was intended more for punishment than for rehabilitation. Conditions within the prison were primitive. Prisoners slept on straw mattresses, although eventually beds were built. Food was meager, usually consisting of cornbread and beans, on good days with bacon. Prisoners were required to work, making everything from harnesses and shoes to barrels and brooms. Diseases spread rapidly, and in 1930, an inmate set a fire during an escape attempt and 322 inmates died in the ensuing fire. After the fire, there were demands for prison reform.

In 1885, the penitentiary became the site for executions in the state. At first, condemned prisoners were executed by hanging, but in 1897 the electric chair replaced the prison's gallows. A total of 315 prisoners, both men and women, were electrocuted before the death penalty was halted in Ohio.

On October 31, 1952, a riot erupted in the chow hall, when prisoners began banging on their cups with spoons to protest the "slop" they were served as food. Prisoners began throwing food, trays, and other utensils. The "Halloween Riot" ended after officers opened fire, killing one prisoner and wounding four others.

37. Gorilla Marketing

John Bushnell Hanna was born on January 2, 1947, in Knoxville, Tennessee. He grew up on his father's farm outside Knoxville, and volunteered as a veterinarian's assistant when he was 11. He attended The Kiski School, an all-boys boarding school in Saltsburg, Pennsylvania, then majored in business and political science at Muskingum College, where he got in trouble for keeping ducks in his dorm room and a donkey in a shed behind his fraternity house. He worked for a wildlife adventure company and directed the small Sanford Zoo and Central Florida Zoo from 1973 to 1975.

When Hanna was offered the position as director of the Columbus Zoo in 1978, the facility consisted of undeveloped land, muddy, smelly exhibit venues, 2 elephants, an outdoor cage of raccoons, a lion or two, and "Colo," a Western lowland gorilla, the first gorilla to be born in captivity.

Nicknamed "Jungle Jack," sporting a khaki safari outfit and deep tan, Hanna proved to be well-suited to public relations for the zoo. From 1981 until 1983, he hosted a television show called *Hanna's Ark* that aired on the local CBS affiliate in Columbus, WBNS. Hanna's live animal demonstrations on *Good Morning America* and *Late Night with David Letterman* brought national attention to the Columbus Zoo. His tenure as director is viewed as largely responsible for elevating its caliber and reputation, and increasing annual attendance by over 400%.

38. Red Boutineer

Dr. Levi L. Lamborn was a physician, horticultural-ist, politician, and prominent resident of Alliance, Ohio. Lamborn had successfully propagated one of the six car-nation seedlings he had imported from France, a variety he named the "Lamborn Red." He was eager to reveal the first carnation to bloom in America to William McKinley, his friend and opponent for the Congressional seat in their district.

On noting how impressed McKinley was with his flower, it is reported that Lamborn removed the fragrant blossom from its stem and placed it in his friend's lapel. McKinley won the election and went on to become Gov-ernor of Ohio, and later President of the United States. He continued to wear a red carnation pushed through the buttonhole of his lapel in all of his subse-quent political campaigns and associated the flower with his success.

In September of 1901 while attending the Pan-American Exposition in Buffalo, New York, President McKinley was wearing a "Lamborn Red" boutineer when he was shot by an assassin's bullet and later died.

After McKinley's death, the Ohio General Assembly passed a joint resolution, naming the red carnation the official Ohio state flower. Each year on his birthday, a bouquet of red carnations is placed at the base of his statue in Columbus.

39. The Lady in Gray

Some 2,260 Confederate prisoners died of disease and malnutrition at Camp Chase (see **Northern Hospitality**, page 53), the prisoner of war camp in what is now the Hilltop neighborhood of Columbus. So it is not surprising that the place has come to be considered haunted.

The legend of the "Lady in Gray" dates back to just after the Civil War, when visitors to Camp Chase would spot a ghostly apparition walking among the seemingly endless rows of tombstones, wearing a flowing gray dress and grey veil which hides her face from view. She appeared to be reading the carved names on the grave markers, perhaps looking for her lost love among the many young Rebel soldiers who died at the camp. She has since been observed walking directly through trees and through the iron cemetery gates.

Some say she is Louisiana Ransburgh Briggs, who in life would go into the cemetery late at night to place flowers on graves of the fallen Confederate soldiers. It seems she has continued the ritual in death. At the tombstone of Benjamin Allen of the 50th Tennessee Volunteers, fresh flowers mysteriously appear on a regular basis.

In the summer of 1988, during a Civil War reenactment, many in the crowd heard the sounds of a woman crying, followed by a huge gust of wind that blew over tables and tents. Was it the Lady in Gray?

40. High Performance Carr

Born in Columbus on October 22, 1880, Joseph F. Carr was the son of Irish immigrants Michael and Margaret Carr. The sixth of seven children, Joseph played a variety of sports while he was growing up in southeast Columbus. His formal education consisted of five years at St. Dominic's Elementary School, and at the age of 13 he went to work at a local machine shop to help support his family. By the age of 20, he was hired as a journeyman machinist at the Panhandle Division of the Pennsylvania Railroad.

In 1907, Carr turned the reborn Columbus Panhandles football team into one of the largest draws in early professional football, starring the Nesser Brothers (see **Handle with Care**, page 46), and were nearly unbeatable at home in Indianola Park (see **Coney Island's Baby**, page 45).

In 1920, Carr helped to form the American Professional Football Association, made up of 14 franchises with the legendary Jim Thorpe as the first league president (later replaced by Carr). In 1922, he instituted a change in name to the National Football League.

Carr moved the league's headquarters to Columbus, drafted a league constitution and by-laws, gave teams territorial rights, developed membership criteria for the franchises, and issued standings, so that the league would have a clear champion.

The NFL's original "Most Valuable Player" award was named for Carr in 1938.

41. The Truth is Out There

The "Big Ear" Radio Telescope was designed and built under the leadership of Dr. John D. Kraus, professor of Electrical Engineering and Astronomy at Ohio State. Located on the grounds of the Perkins Observatory, about 20 miles north of Columbus, the project was part of OSU's Search for Extraterrestrial Intelligence (SETI) project.

On August 15, 1977, astronomer Dr. Jerry R. Ehman was reading a printout of radio data from Ohio State Big Ear Radio Observatory when he discovered a string of code so remarkable that he circled it and scribbled "Wow!" in the margin. The signal bore expected hallmarks of potential non-terrestrial and non-solar system origin. It was observed by the Big Ear for a duration of 72 seconds, but was never detected again.

Since then, the "Wow" signal has stood as one of the central enigmas for alien-hunters. The signal was referenced in the TV series *The X-Files* in the second season opening episode, "Little Green Men." In that episode, Agent Scully investigates the provenance of an unknown radio signal that has sent her partner Agent Mulder off to the SETI installation at Arecibo Observatory in Puerto Rico.

In late 1997, after almost 40 years of operation, Big Ear ceased operation. The land on was sold to land developers who expanded an adjacent 9-hole golf course to 18 holes.

42. Fallen Arches

In September of 1888, the organization of Civil War veterans, the Grand Army of the Republic, held its annual jamboree in Columbus. With more than 250,000 conventioneers descending on the city, huge tent compounds were assembled around the city and dozens of street-spanning wooden arches, illuminated by decorative gaslights, erected along 12 blocks of the High Street parade route. The vets left, but the arches were kept in place, and as the single most identifiable image of the city, Columbus became known as the "Arch City."

In the next few years, local horse-drawn streetcars were replaced by electrified streetcars owned and operated by the Columbus Railway, Power and Light Company. In order to carry electric cables needed to run cars along the major north-south thoroughfare, the company replaced the wooden arches with metal arches, each hung with a looping strand of electric light bulbs. Columbus became "the most brilliantly illuminated city in the country."

In 1914, the arches were torn down and replaced with cluster lights on poles. The era of "Arch City" had come to an end. Then in 2002, nearly ninety years after their removal, seventeen metal archways were installed in the Short North district. A special lighting ceremony was held on September 1, 2007 to commemorate the return of the arches.

43. The Flying Telephone

Born on October 23, 1969, and adopted by John and Joan Resch of Columbus, Tina Resch became the center of the best-documented case of poltergeist activity of the twentieth century.

During the spring of 1984, the Resch home descended into chaos, as fourteen-year-old Tina became the focus of a strange series of events. Appliances turned themselves on without electric current, objects flew through the air, and furniture moved across the floor whenever she was in their presence. Journalists were called in to investigate.

The coverage included a series of color photographs that were taken by newspaper photojournalist Fred Shannon of *The Columbus Dispatch* (see **Breaking News**, page 66) which showed Tina sitting in an armchair with a telephone handset and flexible cable in flight in front of her from left to right. The famous "flying telephone" picture taken by Shannon was circulated by the AP throughout the world. Tina's story, including the now-famous photograph, was featured on a 1993 episode of *Unsolved Mysteries*.

The paranormal events propelled Tina into a downward spiral that led to an abusive marriage, a divorce, and the birth of a child – all before her twentieth birthday. Three years later she was charged with her child's murder, and she is currently serving a life sentence for a crime she maintains she did not commit.

44. Refuse To Lose

In Columbus, his name is still spoken in reverential tones. Born in Clifton, Ohio, on February 14, 1913, Wayne Woodrow "Woody" Hayes played center at Newcomerstown High School in Newcomerstown, Ohio. At Denison University, he played tackle under coach Tom Rogers. After graduating from Denison in 1935, Hayes went on to serve as assistant coach at two Ohio high schools, Mingo Junction and New Philadelphia.

Hayes served as the head coach at Denison University and Miami University before coming to Ohio State, where during his 28 seasons, his teams won three national championships (1954, 1957, 1968), captured 13 Big Ten Conference titles, and amassed a record of 205–61–10.

His basic coaching philosophy was that "nobody could win football games unless they regarded the game positively and would agree to pay the price that success demands of a team."

Although he was venerated practically as a living saint by many citizens of Columbus, Hayes' coaching career ended ingloriously when he was fired after an incident during the 1978 Gator Bowl in which he punched Clemson nose guard player Charlie Bauman, who had returned an interception near the OSU sideline. After the incident, Hayes reflected on his career by saying, "Nobody despises to lose more than I do. That's got me into trouble over the years, but it also made a man of mediocre ability into a pretty good coach."

45. Coney Island's Baby

A local dentist by the name of Charles E. Miles, inspired by the success of Luna Park in Coney Island, partnered with Frederick Ingersoll, an amusement park developer, to create Indianola Park.

Opened to the public on Thursday, June 8, 1905, on the north side of Columbus near the Ohio State campus, the park was just outside of city limits so it was exempt from blue laws that forbade dancing and other amusements on Sundays. It also escaped various taxes, licenses, and fees.

Indianola Park featured a dance pavilion, mammoth swimming pool, roller coaster, carousel, scenic railroad, band shell, and athletic playing fields (see **High Performance Carr**, page 40). Events like balloon ascensions, high wire acts, baby beauty pageants, and fireworks extravaganzas were also part of the park's draw.

The park drew crowds as large as 10,000 on summer weekends, and up to 5,000 people waded into the pool on hot summer days.

In 1927, as radio and motion pictures grew in popularity, the park sold part of its land to the Columbus Board of Education for the construction of Indianola Junior High School, the first junior high school in the United States.

In April 1937, after 32 years of operation, the park declared bankruptcy, and in February 1939, remaining assets were ordered sold to satisfy creditors.

46. Handle With Care

In 1901, local railroad workers formed a professional football team called the Columbus Panhandles, named for the Pennsylvania Railroad route from Pittsburgh to Columbus. Members of the team were mainly European immigrants who learned the game of football on the sandlots of the rail yards.

The team, known by the nickname "Handles," played only two games, but was reorganized in 1907 by Joseph Carr (see **High Performance Carr**, page 40) who recruited what is considered the most unusual family ever to play professional sports, the seven Nesser brothers – Al, Frank, Fred, John, Phil, Ray and Ted. Over the next two decades the Nesser family became the backbone of the Panhandle franchise.

The brothers and their teammates on the Columbus Panhandles worked a 10-hour day, but rushed through lunch so they could practice football for 50 minutes before they returned to their labors. The Nessers averaged more than 210 pounds apiece, in an era in which the average professional lineman weighed about 180 pounds. Notre Dame coach Knute Rockne once said "getting hit by a Nesser is like falling off a moving train." Frank Nesser, whose abilities were compared to those of Jim Thorpe, led the Handles in scoring.

Two of the brothers' sons, John P. and Bill, later played football for Ohio State.

47. Jelly's Partner

In 1890, a St. Louis physician encouraged the owner of a food products company, George A. Bayle Jr., to process and package ground peanut paste as a nutritious protein substitute for people with poor teeth who couldn't chew meat. The physician apparently had experimented by grinding peanuts in his hand-cranked meat grinder. Bayle mechanized the process and began selling peanut butter out of barrels for about 6¢ per pound.

In 1908, Benton Black began the commercial processing of peanut butter in Columbus. Originally, Black operated as "American Refining Company," but there was already a company using the name, and he lost the legal battle over naming rights. To come up with a new name, he reversed the first four letters of "American" and instead of using a "C" for "Company," he used a "K." The brand became "Krema."

Black's slogan was "I refuse to sell outside of Ohio." While that may have seemed like great marketing, it was actually his only practical alternative. Freshly-ground peanut butter, packed in barrels, spoiled very quickly. With a short shelf, Ohio really was the only place he could sell it.

The Krema Nut Company of Columbus is America's oldest peanut butter producer still in operation today. Only the Sanitarium Health Food Company of Australia has been making peanut butter longer.

48. Man Who Would Be President

Rutherford Birchard Hayes was born in Delaware, Ohio, on October 4, 1822, two months after his father died. When the boy was only three, his brother Lorenzo was skating on a frozen pond when the ice cracked and he fell through and drowned. For several years afterwards, Rutherford's mother would not let him play outside.

After graduating from Norwalk Academy, he enrolled in Kenyon College in Gambier, Ohio. He finished at the head of his class, then went on to Harvard Law School, obtaining a law degree in January of 1845. He began the first of his two terms in Congress after the end of the Civil War. He was then elected governor of Ohio. As governor, he helped get blacks the right to vote and helped found the Ohio Agricultural and Mechanical College (see **Seeds of Learning**, page 5).

His successful record in Columbus brought Hayes the Republican presidential nomination in 1876, which pitted him against Samuel J. Tilden of New York. Hayes was elected President in what rivals the 2000 election as the most corrupt contest in the nation's history. The popular vote was 4,300,000 for Tilden to 4,036,000 for Hayes, but with the Electoral College votes of four states contested, Congress established a commission to decide the dispute. Made up of eight Republicans and seven Democrats, the commission determined all the contests in favor of Hayes. He became the 19th President of the United States.

49. Tycoon

William "Billy" Neil, who arrived in Columbus in 1818, just a few years after the city was formed, made a fortune between 1820 and 1860 meeting the transportation needs of most of the Northwest Territory.

His first stagecoach line operated between Columbus and Granville. Eventually, he became known as the "Stagecoach King" with a network of lines from Cumberland, Maryland, to St. Louis, Missouri. In the late 1840s, sensing that times were changing, he built and operated railroads between Columbus and Cleveland, Columbus and Indiana.

In 1827, Neil purchased a 300-acre parcel of land north of Columbus from Joseph Vance, who would later become the 13th Governor of Ohio. This land would ultimately become the site of the Ohio Agricultural and Mechanical College (see **Seeds of Learning**, page 5), now Ohio State University, after Neil donated the land to the state in 1870.

On property across the street from the Ohio State Capitol building, he built an inn called the Neil House in 1839 at a cost of around $100,000. This was the first of three Neil House Hotels that would occupy that land until the last hotel was torn down in the 1970s to make way for the Huntington Tower.

Neil made a practice of carrying a cane made out of a buckeye tree that William Henry Harrison gave him in 1840 (see **Family Tree**, page 29).

50. That's Entertainment

Inspired by France's famous, Palais De Versailles, the Palace Theater opened its doors to Columbus audiences in 1926. The theater was designed by Thomas W. Lamb, architect of New York's Ziegfeld Theatre and the second incarnation of Madison Square Garden. In charge of bookings was impresario Edward Albee of the Keith-Albee vaudeville circuit.

The Theater was originally used mostly to house acts whose performers would reside in Columbus for several days and in some cases for weeks on end. The dressing room tower in the backstage area was designed as a small hotel, complete with a "front desk," where performers picked up their room keys and mail. Kitchen facilities and a children's playroom were provided.

Beginning in the 1930s and continuing through the 1950s, the Palace Theater held the distinction of offering the best quality of entertainment in Columbus. Big name acts like, Bing Crosby, Louis Armstrong, Nat King Cole, Jackie Gleason, Tommy Dorsey, Duke Ellington, Burns & Allen, Jack Benny and Glenn Miller at one time or on several occasions found themselves taking advantage of the amenities offered to those who performed at the Palace.

Today the theater functions as a multi-use performing arts venue, owned and operated by CAPA (The Columbus Association for the Performing Arts).

51. Safe House

Fernando Cortez Kelton was a merchant from Vermont who rose to prominence in Columbus as a drygoods wholesaler. He and his wife, Sophia Langdon Stone Kelton, built the Kelton House, a Greek Revival and Italianate mansion, on Town Street in 1852. The Keltons were fervent abolitionists who used their home as a stop on the Underground Railroad, a network of safe houses used by escaped slaves en route to Canada.

Fernando Kelton, well-known for his abolitionist work, was selected to be a pallbearer at the funeral procession of Abraham Lincoln when the assassinated president's remains were brought to Columbus on their way to Illinois for burial (see **Lincoln on His Way Home**, page 4).

The Keltons' eldest son Oscar was killed in the Civil War Battle of Brice's Crossroads near Baldwyn in Lee County, Mississippi, on June 10, 1864. That same year, the Keltons took in Martha Hartway, a young runaway slave from Virginia who they raised as part of the family.

The house passed on to the Kelton's son, Frank who married Isabella Morrow Coit, a suffragette who was one of the first four women to graduate from Ohio State. Her mother was the local women's rights leader Elizabeth Greer Coit.

Grace Bird Kelton, an interior designer who redecorated the White House for Jacqueline Kennedy, was the last member of the family to own the house.

52. Whistle Blower

The Colsoff Company had manufactured whistles in Columbus since 1956. After entrepreneur Ray Giesse purchased the company in 1987, he changed the name to "American Whistle" to emphasize the fact that his company is the only manufacturer of metal whistles in the United States, and he boosted production from 70,000 whistles to over 1 million annually.

The so-called "pea whistle" was invented by an English soccer referee more than a hundred years ago. The little ball inside ricocheting from one surface to another interferes with the airflow and makes the unique quavering note that demands attention.

All of the local whistles are made of solid brass (an alloy of copper and zinc), producing best tone and resonance quality of any metal, for the same reason that brass is used for musical instruments. American Whistle developed a synthetic material to replace the common cork ball. It behaves like natural cork in every respect except that it does not absorb any moisture. This helps keep the ball from getting stuck inside the whistle and not swirling freely.

American Whistle Company high-decibel "warbling" whistles have become the official whistle of the Boy Scouts of America and the National Fraternal Order of Police. The company makes the NFL commemorative gold-plated whistles for the officiating crew at the Super Bowl, inscribed with the Super Bowl logo and the referees' initials.

53. Northern Hospitality

During the Civil War, Columbus was a major base for the volunteer Union Army, housing 26,000 troops and Confederate prisoners of war at Camp Chase, named for Lincoln's Secretary of the Treasury and former Ohio governor Salmon P. Chase, located at what is now the Hilltop neighborhood.

Four future Presidents visited Camp Chase – Andrew Johnson, Rutherford B. Hayes, James Garfield, and William McKinley. It also held Confederates captured during Morgan's Raid in 1863, including Col. Basil W. Duke.

On oath of honor, Confederate officers were permitted to wander through Columbus, register in hotels, and receive gifts of money and food; a few attended sessions of the state senate. The public paid for camp tours, and Chase became a tourist attraction. When complaints over such lax discipline provoked an investigation, the situation changed.

As the war raged on, conditions became worse. Prisoners were crowded into a confined space, poorly clad, uncomfortably housed, insufficiently fed, and provided scant medical attention. Original facilities for 3,000 men were jammed with close to 10,000. Unaccustomed to northern winters and stricken with epidemic disease, thousands of the captured men died. More than 2,200 are buried in the Camp Chase Cemetery, one of the largest military cemeteries in the North.

54. Three Ring Circus

The Sells brothers of Columbus – Ephraim, Allen, Lewis, and Peter – started out in the auction business, following circus troupes around the country in order to take advantage of the audiences they attracted.

The brothers became fascinated by a man named George Richards, a performer who shot himself out of a cannon. The brothers purchased Richards' act, some cast-off circus equipment, nine cages of animals and two camels, and presented a show in downtown Columbus in the spring of 1871. The show grew steadily, and by 1878 was transported around the country in 47 custom railway cars; by 1890, the Sells Brothers Circus was the second largest circus in America. A typical season would run from mid-April, opening in Columbus, to early December, usually closing in a southern city. In 1884 the circus traveled 11,537 miles.

In 1898, after the death of Ephraim, the eldest brother, James Bailey of Barnum and Bailey and W.W. Cole (of Cole Brothers Circus) each acquired a quarter interest in the enterprise. When Peter and Allen both passed away in 1904, Lewis sold the remaining shares to Bailey for $150,000 cash. Bailey then sold half share of the Sells circus to the Ringling Brothers.

The Columbus headquarters was closed by 1910. The act eventually became part of the conglomerate Ringling Brothers, Barnum and Bailey's Greatest Show on Earth.

55. Song of Ohio

A distant cousin of Ezra Cornell, founder of Cornell University, Columbus-born Fred Cornell was an all-around athlete at Ohio State. On the track team he ran relays, the 100-yard dash, low and high hurdles; he was the starting center on the basketball team, starting shortstop on the baseball team, and reserve end on the football team. He was also a member of the Men's Glee Club, an amateur poet, and the composer of the words to a song that would become the Ohio State alma mater.

There are varying accounts as to when and where he actually wrote the words. It was either in 1902 on a train returning home from a football game in Ann Arbor, an 86-0 defeat at the hands of Michigan (see **Muck Fichigan!** page 17), to this day the worst loss in school history. Or it may have been a year later at the request of the Glee Club. Both versions agree that it was sung publicly for the first time by the Glee Club in 1903.

The word "Carmen" means "song or poem" in Spanish, and the melody was borrowed from *Spanish Chant*, an ancient hymn. Cornell borrowed a few of his words from the Yale song, *Bright College Years* (the OSU football coach, Perry Hale, was a former captain of the Yale football team).

Cornell went on to a successful career in the automobile and shipbuilding industries. In 1961 he received the University's Distinguished Service Award for his composition of "Carmen Ohio."

56. "Spirit of Columbus"

In 1937, Amelia Earhart attempted to fly around the world, but her plane was lost on the flight between New Guinea and Howland Island. Twenty-seven years later, a woman from Columbus, flying an 11-year-old Cessna 180 single-engine monoplane she christened "The Spirit of Columbus," became the first woman to successfully complete Earhart's around-the-world route.

Geraldine "Jerrie" Fredritz Mock, born on November 22, 1925, in Newark, Ohio, caught the flying bug at age 7, after a 15-minute ride in a Ford "Tin Goose." She attended Ohio State as the only woman then enrolled in its aeronautical engineering program. When she took her first flying lesson in 1956, it was obvious that she was a natural pilot. She soloed after only nine hours and 15 minutes of instruction.

Jerrie was called the "flying housewife," since she had 3 children when she announced plans to fly around the world. *The Columbus Dispatch* (see **Breaking News**, page 66) agreed to fund most of the trip. She took off from Columbus, at 9:31 AM on March 19, 1964, and landed back in Columbus on April 18. The flight took a total of 30 days, with 21 stopovers, 22,858 miles in flight, and just over 158 flying hours.

"The Spirit of Columbus" was displayed in National Air and Space Museum General Aviation Gallery until 1984 and is now stored at the Garber Facility.

57. Into the Mirror

At one time Mirror Lake was a source of drinking water for both the Ohio State campus and residents living nearby. Originally fed by a spring, but with encroaching campus development, the lake all but dried up in the 1920s. The city's municipal system now pumps water into the lake.

At the turn of the last century, "May Festival," later called "May Week," was the university's biggest showcase of school pride. Students saw it as a time to prove class dominance, with upperclassmen dunking freshmen in the lake, often a part of initiation by a group called "Bucket & Dipper." The tradition of dunking students in Mirror Lake lasted until the late 1960s.

Eventually, "May Week" took on less importance and "Beat Michigan Week" took on more. In 1990, after an OSU marching band-led torchlight parade ended with a rally outside of Pomerene Hall near Mirror Lake, several students spontaneously jumped into the lake. It was the beginning of the Thursday night ritual of a mass jump into Mirror Lake prior to the annual football game between OSU and Michigan (see **Muck Fichigan!** page 17).

Mirror Lake is currently an artificially maintained system. A brick floor that was added to the bottom of the lake prevents infiltration of groundwater. Stone mortar banks are vertical walls that do not allow for the growth of natural vegetation.

58. Golden Bear

Born in Columbus on January 21, 1940, Jack William Nicklaus, the son of a local pharmacist, was raised in the suburb of Upper Arlington and attended Upper Arlington High School. Overcoming a mild case of polio as a child, he took up golf at the age of 10, shooting a 51 at Scioto Country Club for his first nine holes ever played. By age 12, he won the first of 6 straight Ohio State Junior titles. While attending Ohio State University, he won the U.S. Amateur Championship twice, and an NCAA Championship.

Nicklaus turned pro in 1962, earning $33.33 in his first event as a pro. Over the course of his 25-year period of 100 major championships as a professional, Nicklaus finished either first or second 36 times, in the top three 45 times, the top five 54 times, and the top ten 67 times. Nicklaus brought power to the forefront in golf, being the longest driver of his generation, but he also was one of the best clutch putters ever, and his concentration skills were legendary. In the mid-1960s, after helping Pete Dye with the development of The Golf Club in New Albany (see **Stay the Course**, page 14), he started his own firm, eventually involved in the design of 271 courses.

He once famously said, "It's hard not to play golf that's up to Jack Nicklaus standards when you are Jack Nicklaus."

59. Towering Achievement

In 1927, the American Insurance Union, an eccentric combination of insurance company, secret society and social club, built a headquarters they called "The Citadel" at 50 West Broad Street. At 555 ½ feet, it was the tallest building between New York and Chicago, and reigned as the tallest building in Columbus until the Rhodes State Office Tower was built in 1973. The building is extremely stable because the foundation goes all the way down to bedrock, a system derived from the method used to build the foundations for the towers of the Brooklyn Bridge.

By 1935, AIU, forced into bankruptcy by the Great Depression, sold the building to a group led by Leslie L. LeVeque, the designer of an automatic pinsetter for bowling alleys known as the "Columbus Pinsetter" and developer of Olentangy Park (see **Almost Disneyland**, page 18).

The building is festooned with eagles, arcane symbols and figures of people from ancient mythology and the ritual of AIU. Much of the original statuary was removed because it began to crumble and fall into the street below. A 20-foot statue of Colossus was removed so Mr. LeVeque could have a better view from his office windows. The spaces left by the departed sculpture serve as the bases for lights used to illuminate the tower, normally lit in white, but color is added frequently for special occasions.

60. "Old Iron Pants"

Born in Columbus on November 15, 1906, Curtis Emerson LeMay was the son of Erving LeMay, an iron-worker and general handyman who never held a job for more than a few months. The family moved around the country as his father looked for work, as far away as Montana and California, eventually returning to Columbus.

LeMay attended Columbus public schools, then worked his way through Ohio State, graduating with a bachelor's degree in civil engineering. He was commissioned in the United States Army Air Corps in January 1930, becoming one of the first members of the Air Corps to receive specialized training in aerial navigation.

He became an outstanding air combat leader during World War II, developing bombardment tactics and strategies that left Nazi Germany in rubble. He was transferred to the Pacific theater, where he took over command of the B-29s and led the air war against Japan. LeMay incinerated every major Japanese city and oversaw the dropping of the atomic bombs. He was fondly known among his troops as "Old Iron Pants" throughout his career.

During the Cuban Missile Crisis in 1962, LeMay clashed with President John F. Kennedy and Defense Secretary McNamara, arguing that he should be allowed to bomb nuclear missile sites in Cuba. In 1968 he was the vice-presidential candidate on the third-party ticket headed by George Wallace. The old warrior died on October 1, 1990.

61. Toontown

Shortly after his 1898 high school graduation, Chillicothe, Ohio, native William Addison "Billy" Ireland was hired by *The Columbus Dispatch* (see **Breaking News**, page 66), where he worked his entire life, drawing four to seven editorial cartoons every week from 1898 to 1935. He had several books published, and he mentored many younger cartoonists including Milton Caniff and Noel Sickles. He turned down syndication contracts and several job offers from larger metropolitan newspapers, explaining that he did not want to leave Columbus.

Ireland was best known for *The Passing Show*, which debuted on February 9, 1908, with its title inspired by George Lederer's *The Passing Show* (1894), the first successful American revue-format entertainment. In his Sunday strip, he commented on everything from local politics and visiting celebrities to the trials and tribulations of the Ohio State football team. For the September 30, 1923, *Passing Show* page, he created a character inspired by Ohio State's 1902 school song, "Carmen Ohio." *The Passing Show* came to an end on June 2, 1935, the Sunday following his death on May 29.

Ohio State received a gift of $1 million from Jean Schulz, the widow of *Peanuts* creator Charles M. Schulz, to support the renovation of Sullivant Hall as the home of the world's most comprehensive academic research facility dedicated to documenting printed cartoon art, the Billy Ireland Cartoon Library & Museum.

62. The King of Cards

Born in Columbus on July 20, 1869, Howard Thurston was inspired as a small boy by Alexander Herrmann, the most famous magician of the era. After attending a local performance by Herrmann in Columbus, Thurston was determined to follow his footsteps in the entertainment business. He first toured the United States with a small act. Then a European vaudeville tour started him on the road to fame. Thurston's financial success in Europe let him build an illusion show which he took around the world, billing himself as the "King of Cards."

He visited Australia, India, and the Far East, polishing his skills and developing lavish 3-hour shows. New effects were added every year as old ones were retired. While his original fame rested on card manipulations, Thurston's later reputation was earned with large stage illusions. One of his tricks was to make an Overland Whippet automobile disappear. He also was famous for floating an assistant above the stage and out over the footlights where she eventually vanished without a trace.

From 1908 until 1936, the year of his death, Howard Thurston was acknowledged as the "World's Master" on the secrets of magic tricks. He had the largest traveling magic show for the time, requiring more than eight entire train cars to transport his props across the country. He is entombed in the mausoleum at Green Lawn Abbey (see **Final Resting Place**, page 24).

63. Die Nachbarschaft

German immigrants who settled on pastures and farmlands in South Columbus, most arriving during a twenty year period from 1840 to 1860, comprised as much as a third of the population of the entire city at that time. This close knit group, mostly brick and stone mason and brewers, kept their culture intact by speaking German in the schools and churches they built as well as publishing German language newspapers.

German Village is rooted in brick buildings and brick-paved streets made from "vitrified block." Harder and stronger than ordinary construction brick, vitrified material required special types of clay, and the best was a silica-rich material called shale, of which Ohio enjoys a natural abundance. The earliest vitrified bricks supplied to the city of Columbus were made by the Malvern Clay Company near Canton.

Louis Hoster was the first brewer among the German immigrants. In 1836, a year after arriving in Columbus, Hoster opened the first local brewery. Over the next three decades, the thirsty city required five more breweries keep up with demand. According to records, during the 1880s Columbus had fifty churches but as many as six hundred saloons.

Prohibition devastated the work force by closing breweries, one of the main sources of income for German, leading to the gradual dissolution of the German community.

64. Salad Days

In 1896, Italian immigrant Teresa Marzetti arrived in Columbus from her native Florence. Within a year she established a small restaurant on Broad Street called Marzetti's, a local favorite especially among Ohio State students in its early years.

Customers who enjoyed Teresa's creamy coleslaw and salad dressings were often seen leaving the restaurant with bottles of their favorites. By 1947, the dressings had become so popular that the restaurant's second floor kitchen was converted into a full-scale factory, and the Marzetti brand of salad dressings found its way into grocery stores throughout Ohio. In 1955, as demand increased, production moved to a separate facility on Indianola Avenue.

During the 1920s, Teresa came up with a dish she called the "Johnny Marzetti," named after her brother-in-law. A baked casserole, the dish included ground beef, cheese, tomato sauce, and pasta noodles. The dish is still served at social gatherings and in school lunchrooms throughout the Midwest.

When Teresa Marzetti died in 1972, the restaurant closed, however, the salad dressing brand had been sold two years earlier to the Specialty Food Group of Lancaster Colony Corporation, adding Marzetti's to their Cardini's, Girard's, Mamma Bella, and Sister Schubert's brands. Today, sales of Marzetti's products exceeds $200 million a year.

65. Snake Oil Salesman

Born on a Pennsylvania Farm in 1830, Samuel Brubaker Hartman worked his way through medical school at the Cincinnati Farmer's College by selling German bibles to immigrants. In 1890, he abandoned his medical practice to produce a "medicine" called Peruna which would make him a millionaire many times over.

In 1895, Dr. Hartman hired his son-in-law, Frederick W. Schumacher, to promote the cure-all tonic. Schumacher spent $1 million annually for ads that promoted Peruna as a cure for erysipelas, bunions, dyspepsia, heat rash, fever and consumption. He also claimed it would prevent loss of hair, smallpox, sunstroke, near-sightedness, and old age. Peruna became the best selling tonic in America and Hartman became the wealthiest man in Columbus.

Actually, Peruna was basically a variation of diluted cheap vermouth, low grade gin, and questionable bitters, plus a few other benign ingredients in small amounts. After the Internal Revenue Service required retailers who sold it to hold a liquor license, sales fell off sharply.

Hartman spent his declining years on an elegant 5,000-acre farm south of Columbus, which was stocked with fancy breeds of cattle, horses, and poultry. His empire eventually came to an end in the 1940s.

66. Breaking News

Pooling a total of $900, ten Columbus printers (William Trevitt Jr., Samuel Bradford, Timothy McMahon, James O'Donnell, Peter Johnson, L.P. Stephens, John M. Webb, J.S.B. Owen, C.M. Morris, and Willoughby W. Webb), launched *The Daily Dispatch* on July 1, 1871. The inaugural edition of the afternoon publication consisted of four pages and sold for 3 cents.

In April 1895, the afternoon publication moved to larger quarters at Gay and High Streets. On December 17, 1899, *The Dispatch* published its first Sunday edition, by then the dominant newspaper in Columbus. The newspaper changed hands many times in its early years until 1905, when brothers Harry Preston Wolfe and Robert Frederick Wolfe (see **Wolfe Pack**, page 27) bought what by then was called *The Columbus Evening Dispatch*. The Wolfe brothers, sons of Andrew Jackson Wolfe, a Civil War veteran and local shoemaker, had entered the publishing business two years earlier, with the purchase of *The Ohio State Journal*.

In November 1925, the paper moved to 34 South Third Street. Over the decades, the building was enlarged several times to accommodate a growing staff and new presses, the last of which were installed in 1971, the paper's centennial year. *The Columbus Evening Dispatch* became *The Columbus Dispatch* in 1975. Just over a decade later, the newspaper moved to the morning market, publishing its first early edition on January 1, 1986.

67. Hop Along

Born in Columbus on March 2, 1934, Howard Albert Cassady attended Central High School (now-closed) and routinely snuck into Ohio Stadium. At 5-foot-10, 170-pounds, he played baseball in high school and didn't consider football until he enrolled at Ohio State.

Cassady earned the nickname "Hopalong" during his first game as a freshman. A local sportswriter said he "hopped all over the field like the performing cowboy," a reference to the fictional character Hopalong Cassidy, created in 1904 by Clarence E. Mulford and popularized by William Boyd in TV westerns. In that game, Cassady came off the bench to score three touchdowns in a win over Indiana University. During his college career, Cassady scored 37 touchdowns in 36 games; he also played baseball, leading the team in home runs in 1955 and in stolen bases in 1956.

In 1955, Cassady won the Heisman Trophy (by the largest margin at the time), the Maxwell Award, and was named the Associated Press Athlete of the Year. He went on to play nine seasons in the National Football League: seven for the Detroit Lions, and one each for the Cleveland Browns and the Philadelphia Eagles.

In retirement he served as a scout for the New York Yankees baseball team, and as the first base coach for their former AAA affiliate, the Columbus Clippers.

68. Sleep Cheap

Born in Cleveland on May 25, 1935, James R. Trueman attended Ohio State, and after a stint in the military, he became a developer of apartments, office buildings, and mobile home parks. Anticipating a growing market for budget travel lodging, in 1972 Trueman opened the first Red Roof Inn in the Columbus suburb of Grove City with a single room rate of $8.50. The concept was successful, and today the chain has 345 locations in 36 states and employs nearly 6,000 people. Except in a few locations where zoning or building codes interfered, all the motels featured the chain's signature red roofs.

The original slogan was "Sleep Cheap," but as Red Roof Inn's prices increased due to inflation, room rates were considered too high to be cheap. The slogan was changed to "Hit The Roof."

Early in 1990, Red Roof Inns developed its first full-service hotel, including restaurant, indoor swimming pool, health club, and conference center, near company headquarters in Columbus. The upscale, 182-room hotel was named the Trueman Club, after the company founder. (In 2002 the Trueman Club Hotel became Clarion Hotel & Suites).

Trueman, a sportsman who also owned the TrueSports auto racing team, guided Red Roof Inns until his death in 1986. In 1993, the Morgan Stanley Real Estate Fund acquired the company for $600 million.

69. The General

When the Ohio State basketball team, including future Hall of Fame players Jerry Lucas and John Havlicek (see **Hondo**, page 94), won their only national championship in 1960, teammate Bobby Knight sat on the bench.

Robert Montgomery Knight was born in Massillon, Ohio, on October 25, 1940, the only child of the local freight agent on the railroad line and the second-grade teacher at Walnut Street Elementary in nearby Orrville. Bobby played basketball, football and baseball for the Orrville Red Riders, but he lived for basketball. He went on to play college basketball for the Buckeyes, but was a starter in only two games.

After college, Knight became a high school coach in Cuyahoga Falls, Ohio, then joined the Army to coach the U.S. Military Academy team at West Point. In 1971, he was hired by Indiana University where he coached the basketball team for 29 years. In 1976, the Hoosiers were undefeated at 32-0 and won the national championship, beating Michigan 86-68 in the title game. In reference to his previous position at West Point, Knight was nicknamed "The General" by broadcaster Dick Vitale.

Although Knight is the only coach to win the NCAA, the NIT, the Olympic Gold and the Pan-Am Gold, he was one of college basketball's most controversial coaches with a history of chair-throwing, referee baiting and run-ins with school officials.

70. Jewel Box

After fire destroyed a number of downtown Columbus theaters between 1889 and 1893, a group of businessmen called for the construction of a "fireproof" venue for theatrical touring productions. Designed in European "jewel box" style by the local architectural firm of Dauben, Krumm, and Riebel, construction began in 1894 on The Great Southern Fireproof Hotel and Opera House at the corner of High and Main Streets.

One of the first commercial facilities in Columbus to use electricity, the Southern opened on September 21, 1896, and the adjacent hotel opened the following summer. Constructed of "fireproof" tile, brick, iron, steel, and concrete, the theater, originally seating 1,723 on three levels, featured plush seats, stylish boxes, excellent sight lines, and absence of posts or other obstructions.

The Southern's first show was a Broadway touring production of *In Gay New York*, followed by *An American Beauty* starring Lillian Russell. Over the years, the greatest names of the theater and vaudeville played the Southern, including Lionel and Ethel Barrymore, Maude Adams, Sarah Bernhardt, Anna Pavalova, Isadora Duncan, John Philip Sousa, Al Jolson, George M. Cohan, Mae West, and W.C. Fields.

Closed in 1979, the theatre was restored in 1998 by the Columbus Association for the Performing Arts during an intensive 14 month restoration process.

71. Fast Eddie

Born in Columbus on October 8, 1890, to German-speaking Swiss immigrants, Edward Vernon Rickenbacker's schooling ended in seventh grade after the accidental death of his father. The boy found jobs to help support his family, and driven by an admiration for machines, went to work at the Columbus Buggy Company (see **Mass Production**, page 8), after it went into the car business, as a trouble-shooter for customers with mechanical problems.

From his job road-testing cars in Columbus, he made his way into automobile racing, setting a world speed record of 134 MPH at Daytona in 1914. When the U.S. entered World War I, he enlisted in the Air Force, becoming America's top scoring fighter ace with 26 confirmed "kills," frequently battling the famed "Red Baron," Manfred von Richthofen.

After returning from the war as a hero, he raised $700,000 to purchase the Indianapolis Speedway, and from 1928 until 1938, he was a Vice-President of General Motors, promoting the company's aeronautic interests. In 1938 he purchased Eastern Airlines and became President until stepping down in 1953 to become Chairman of the Board until his retirement in 1963.

Fred MacMurray played Rickenbacker in the 1945 film *Captain Eddie*. Columbus' Lockbourne Airbase was renamed Rickenbacker Airbase after his death in 1973.

72. Original Balloon Boy

Born in San Francisco on July 9, 1892, Cromwell Dixon's mother moved the family to Columbus when the boy was two years of age. In 1905, after taking a dirigible ride at the Ohio State Fair, young Cromwell began building his own dirigible in the garage behind 221 West 11th Avenue.

On June 9, 1907, fifteen-year-old boy took to the skies in a contraption consisting of a lemon-shaped, coal gas-filled balloon (35 feet long and 17 feet in diameter), powered by Cromwell himself riding a bicycle mounted to the undercarriage.

Before an astonished crowd at Driving Park Racetrack, Cromwell climbed to an altitude of 200 feet and pedaled around the neighborhood for over an hour. With the story carried by newspapers across the country, he was in demand to exhibit the craft. Cromwell and the "Sky Cycle" became a featured attraction at fairs and air shows around the Midwest and as far away as Boston and St. Louis.

In August 1911, Cromwell received his pilot's license, making him the youngest pilot in the world. He spent the next two months demonstrating the Curtiss biplane at events across the West. On September 30, 1911, 19-year-old Cromwell became the first pilot to fly over the Rocky Mountains. Two days later, he was killed when his plane crashed during an exhibition flight at the Washington Interstate Fair in Spokane.

73. The House That Harley Built

Charles William Harley was born in Chicago (hence the nickname "Chic") and his family moved to Columbus, when he was 12 years old. He attended East High in Columbus and became one of the greatest high school football players in Ohio history. The family was to return to Chicago just before Harley's senior year, but the Columbus East principal convinced the family to let Harley stay for his final year. In his athletic career at East High School, Harley's team lost only one game, his last. So many people wanted to see Harley play that football games at East High's now-named "Harley Field" often outdrew Ohio State football games.

Harley came to Ohio State in 1916, leading the Buckeyes to the very first Big Ten championship in school history, finishing 7-0. The following year's record of 8-0-1 gave the Buckeyes a second outright title. In 1918, Harley left to become a pilot in the Air Force during World War I. With his return in 1919, the Buckeyes would only lose one game – to Illinois.

In Harley's era, the Buckeyes played in Ohio Field, which had a seating capacity of no more than 20,000. Harley's exploits so excited the fans of Ohio State football that he inspired a $1.3 million funding drive, starting in 1920, to build massive Ohio Stadium (see **Monument to College Football**, page 35). Nestled snugly on the banks of the Olentangy River, the stately stadium is one of the most recognizable landmarks in all of college athletics.

74. Immortalized in Bronze

In 1955, Columbus established a "Sister City" relationship with Genoa, Italy. To commemorate this relationship, Columbus received a 20-foot, 7,000-pound, bronze statue of Christopher Columbus, sculpted by native Italian artist Edoardo Alfieri, as a gift from Genoa. The legendary explorer holds a rolled document while his proper left hand rests on his chest; he is dressed in a cloak. It was installed on a pedestal overlooking Broad Street in front of Columbus City Hall, dedicated on Columbus Day, October 12, 1955, with an estimated crowd of 200,000 on hand.

Words of gratitude recited at ceremony by legendary Columbus Mayor Maynard Edward "Jack" Sensenbrenner (see **Spizzerinctum**, page 2) and inscribed on the statue's base, convey today an acutely ironic comment on the relative strengths of political correctness and holiday tradition. Sensenbrenner greeted the sculpture, in his words, "We shall ever cherish and be guided by its meaning." Since then, Columbus has established seven other Sister City relationships.

In the mid-1980s, Mayor Dana Rinehart tried to give away Roy Lichtenstein's (see **Pop Art**, page 97) controversial sculpture, "Brushstrokes in Flight" (located at Port Columbus International Airport), to Genoa as a return gift for a statue of Christopher Columbus. It was established that Rinehart didn't have the authority to take such action, so it remains in Columbus.

75. Dotting the "I"

The Script Ohio is a trademark formation devised by OSU band director Eugene J. Weigel, who based the looped design on the marquee sign of the Loew's Ohio Theatre in downtown Columbus. The dotting of the "i," performed before home games, is one of the most beloved traditions in college football.

The band first forms a triple Block O formation, then slowly unwinds to form the letters while playing Robert Planquette's *Le Régiment de Sambre et Meuse*. The drum major leads the outside O into a peel-off movement around the curves of the script, every musician in continual motion. Slowly the three blocks unfold into a long singular line which loops around, creating the word "Ohio." Trumpeter John Brungart dotted the first Script Ohio "i" on October 10, 1936. Since then, a player from the sousaphone (tuba) section has been selected to stand as the dot.

Besides Brungart, only six non-sousaphonists have ever dotted the "i." Honorary dotters have included Bob Hope, Woody Hayes (see **Refuse to Lose**, page 44), OSU President Novice Fawcett, retired ticket director Robert Ries, Jack Nicklaus (see **The Golden Bear**, page 58), and Senator John Glenn. (OSU President Gordon Gee, retired directors Dr. Paul Droste, Jack Evans, and Heavyweight Champion Buster Douglas (see **Knockout**, page 25) have dotted the "i" with the Alumni Band).

76. Stick It To Teflon

It was an Ohio State-educated chemist who invented "the housewife's best friend." Born in New Carlisle, Ohio, on June 26, 1910, Roy J. Plunkett graduated from Manchester College with a degree in Chemical Engineering in 1932. After receiving a Ph.D. at OSU in 1936, Plunkett was hired as a research chemist by E.I. du Pont de Nemours and Company at their Jackson Laboratory in Deepwater, New Jersey.

On April 6, 1938, he made an accidental discovery. Plunkett was playing around with different gases in his lab. His goal was to come up with a better coolant gas. He left one batch of this gas overnight in a container. When he returned the following day, the gas had turned into a waxy solid which he found to be extremely heat-tolerant and stick-resistant.

Known by its trade name, Teflon was introduced commercially in 1949 and has become an important coating for everything from satellite components to cookware.

In 2006, a panel of scientists selected by the Environmental Protection Agency concluded that a perfluorochemical used in Teflon is a likely cancer-causing agent. Oops! Within two to five minutes on a stove, cookware coated with Teflon can exceed temperatures at which the coating breaks apart and emits toxic particles and gases linked to thousands of pet bird deaths and an unknown number of human illnesses each year.

77. Rodeo Drive of the Midwest

At the conclusion of World War II, American families began leaving inner cities, moving to suburbs. Improvements in transportation, the development of interstates during the 1950s, and the increasing accessibility of cars, all spurred this movement from the cities to outlying neighborhoods.

As Americans moved from the cities to suburbs, business owners began to develop shopping centers to attract suburbanites. In 1948, the Town and Country Shopping Center opened in suburban Columbus, regarded as one of the first modern shopping centers in America. In succeeding years, Northland, Eastland and Westland malls, Columbus City Center, and the Mall at Tuttle Crossing became staples for local shoppers. Then came Easton Town Center.

Designed to look like a classic American main street, with public spaces, fountains, a street grid, and metered storefront parking, Easton is the brainstorm of Les Wexner, the founder, chairman and CEO of nearby Limited Brands (see **Unlimited Possibilities**, page 34).

The demise of Planet Hollywood, intended to be a major attraction at Easton, provided an early blow to the project, however, the developers refocused and retooled. The trend-setting "lifestyle" center has become an established part of the Columbus landscape with its own exit on I-270.

78. One Leg at a Time

From the first kickoff in September to the last play in November, life in Columbus seems to revolve around Ohio State football. It all began in the spring of 1890, when George Cole, an undergraduate, persuaded Alexander S. Lilley to coach a football team the university. The Buckeyes first game, on May 3, 1890, against Ohio Wesleyan, was a victory.

OSU's first home game took place on November 1, 1890, against the University of Wooster, in what was then called Recreation Park. The weather was perfect, and the crowd cheered loudly. Nonetheless, the lads of OSU were drubbed soundly by Wooster, 64–0. Over the next eight years, under a number of coaches, the team played to a cumulative record of 31 wins, 39 losses, and 2 ties.

When one of the early coaches, Francis "Close the Gates of Mercy" Schmidt, was asked about the team's chances of beating rival Michigan (see **Muck Fichigan!** page 17), he replied, "They put their pants on one leg at a time same as everyone else." Ever since then, the "Golden Pants Club" has awarded a gold lapel pin shaped like football pants to each OSU Buckeye who has scored a victory over the Wolverines.

Because Schmidt's teams were known for trick plays involving multiple laterals and non-standard tackle-eligible (and even guard-eligible) formations, the press labeled Schmidt's approach as the "razzle-dazzle offense."

79. Johnny Appleseed

The next time you bite into a locally-grown apple, thank John Chapman. Born on September 26, 1774, and raised on a small farm on Leominster, Massachusetts, the young boy's favorite place was the family apple orchard. When he grew up he made it his life's work to plant fruit trees in the developing parts of the country, providing the means for the first settlers to grow their own apples, and apples meant subsistence and self-reliance.

Apple trees are not native to North America; they were brought here by European settlers, as they struggled to establish farms and homes on the frontier. Fresh apples and apple butter were staples in settlers' diets; boiled apple cider and vinegar enabled them to preserve foods. Apple cider (what we today call hard cider) could be traded for flour, sugar, livestock, and other staples in cash-poor settlements. No other fruit could be started so easily, and none could be put to so many essential uses.

By 1801, Chapman was known as "Johnny Appleseed," as he transported 16 bushels of apple seeds from western Pennsylvania down the Ohio River. He had acquired more than 1,000 acres of farmland on which he developed many of the state's first apple orchards and nurseries.

Today, Ohio is ranked 11th among the 35 states that grow apples, with the state's farmers producing some 77,000 pounds of apples each year.

80. Precision Paul

Born in Norwalk, Ohio, on September 7, 1908, Paul Eugene Brown graduated from Washington High School in Massillon in 1925, having played varsity quarterback. Enrolling at Ohio State as a freshman quarterback, Brown found his 145-pound frame would not stand the rigors of major college football, and transferred to Miami (Ohio) University. He completed his academic career in 1940 when he received an M.A. in Education from Ohio State.

His coaching career began in 1930 at the Severn Prep School in Maryland. Two years later, at age 23, he became head football coach of his hometown Massillon Washington High School Tigers. Over nine seasons Brown posted an 80-8-2 record which included a 35-game winning streak. He moved into the college ranks by becoming head coach of the Ohio State Buckeyes in 1941. Under Brown, the Buckeyes went 18–8–1. His players were known for speed, intelligence, and contact; his teams for execution and fundamentals; and he was dubbed "Precision Paul" at Ohio State.

After World War II, he became part-owner and head coach of a Cleveland-based team in the upstart All-America Football Conference dubbed "Browns" in recognition of Paul Brown as an established and popular figure in Ohio sports.

Brown is considered the "father of the modern offense," and one of the greatest of football coaches in history.

81. Stephen King of Pre-Teen Set

Born in Columbus on October 8, 1943, Robert Lawrence Stine grew up in suburban Bexley, using an old typewriter he found in the attic to produce stories and little joke books he gave away at school. He attended Ohio State University, where he became editor of *The Sundial*, the university's humor magazine. In order to fulfill his dream of working as a writer in New York City, he decided to remain in Columbus in order to save up enough money for the move. After a brief stint teaching social studies at a local junior high school, he moved to the big city where he began writing for young audiences, with work for *Junior Scholastic Magazine* and on books like *101 Silly Monster Jokes* and *Bozos on Patrol*.

Stine created and edited the comedy magazine *Bananas* before turning to teen horror with his 1986 novel *Blind Date*. He began the *Fear Street* series in 1989, and then in 1992 launched the unprecedented best-selling *Goosebumps*, which sold more than 220 million copies. Producers later turned Goosebumps into a television series for children.

Like J.K. Rowling, Stine has been credited with encouraging young readers, while at the same time he has weathered criticism for writing stories based on the occult. Non-juvenile works by Stine include his autobiography, *It Came from Ohio! My Life as a Writer*, published in 1997.

82. Johnny Cash's Favorite Singer

Born on October 23, 1956, in Pikeville, Kentucky, the son of Ruth Ann, a key-punch operator, and David Yoakam, a gas-station owner, Dwight David Yoakam was raised in Columbus. During his high school years he excelled in both music and drama, regularly securing the lead role in school plays, such as "Charlie" in a stage version of *Flowers for Algernon*, honing his skills under the guidance of teacher-mentors Jerry McAfee (music) and Charles Lewis (drama); outside of school, he sang and played guitar with local garage bands. After graduating from Northland High School, he briefly attended Ohio State, but dropped out to become a recording artist.

Popular since the early 1980s, Yoakam has recorded more than twenty-one albums and compilations, has charted more than thirty singles on the *Billboard* Hot Country Songs charts, and sold more than 25 million records. His song "Readin', Rightin', Route 23" pays tribute to his childhood move from Kentucky, and is named after a local expression describing the route that rural Kentuckians took to take to find a job outside of the coal mines. (U.S. Route 23 runs north from Kentucky through Columbus and onto the automotive centers of Michigan).

Yoakam has also appeared in films, most notably as the abusive alcoholic Doyle in Billy Bob Thornton's *Sling Blade* and as a psychotic killer in *Panic Room*.

83. The Case for Sausage

Born near Sugar Ridge, Ohio, on May 30, 1918, the son of grocery store owners Stanley and Elizabeth Lewis Evans, Robert Evans worked in the family business, attended schools, and toiled as a newspaper carrier for *The Columbus Dispatch* (see **Breaking News**, page 66). With hopes of a career in veterinary medicine, he attended Ohio State from 1937 to 1939, but left school due to chronic migraine headaches. With career aspirations dashed, Evans returned to Gallipolis and accepted a position as a meat salesman for the Evans Packing Company, another enterprise created by his father and uncles. In 1940, he married Jewell Waters; they had six children.

In 1945, after the war, he returned home with an honorable discharge and opened a 12-seat, 24-hour restaurant at a truck terminal in Gallipolis, where he decided to make his own sausage. Starting with $1,000 ($500 of his and $500 from his father), three hogs, 40 pounds of black pepper, 50 pounds of sage and a few other ingredients, Bob got started in the sausage business, operating on a farm in Bidwell in 1948. Before long, he opened other restaurants, promoting home-style meals, breakfast, and the signature sausage.

By the end of the 20th Century, Bob Evans had become something of a living legend in Ohio due to his restaurants, his Stetson hat, and string tie. By 2010, his company earned $1.75 billion in sales in 713 full-service Bob Evans Restaurants in 18 states.

84. Historian Who Made History

Born in Columbus on October 15, 1917, the son of Arthur M. Schlesinger Sr., an influential social historian at Ohio State University, Arthur M. Schlesinger Jr. attended the Phillips Exeter Academy in New Hampshire and received his first degree at the age of twenty from Harvard, graduating summa cum laude. In 1940, at the age of twenty-three, he was appointed to a fellowship at Harvard. His book, *The Age of Jackson*, was awarded the Pulitzer Prize in 1945.

In 1952, Schlesinger became the primary speech-writer for Illinois Governor Adlai E. Stevenson, the Democratic candidate for President of the United States. In 1960, he supported the nomination of Senator John F. Kennedy of Massachusetts.

After the election, he served as special assistant and "court historian" to President Kennedy from 1961 to 1963. After Kennedy was assassinated on November 22, 1963, Schlesinger wrote a detailed account of the Kennedy Administration, from the transition period to the president's state funeral, titled *A Thousand Days*, winning him his second Pulitzer in 1965. In 1968, he actively supported the presidential campaign of Senator Robert F. Kennedy until Kennedy's assassination in the Ambassador Hotel on June 5, 1968, and wrote the biography *Robert Kennedy and His Times* several years later.

85. Bear Minimum

It was the first self-serve supermarket in the Midwest, and the first supermarket in the country to use cashier-operated motorized conveyor belts. The original Big Bear Store was opened by Wayne E. Brown on February 15, 1934 on West Lane Avenue in Columbus in what was once a dance hall and roller skating rink.

Big Bear was a pioneer in establishing supermarket service departments, developing a strong reputation for its high quality produce, meat, deli and bakery departments. Shopping carts were introduced in 1937. Big Bear's private brand, "Betty Brown," was named after the founder's wife. For many years, the store's orange and blue "Buckeye" trading stamps were a familiar sight for shoppers.

In 1954, a new prototype store was opened at the Graceland Shopping Center. With an interior store layout that became an industry standard, the store featured perishable items in the center of the stores and lower displays to highlight products. "Big Bear Plus" stores were among the first superstores combining a supermarket with a general merchandise store.

The Columbus-based chain, having grown to 70 Big Bear and Big Bear Plus stores in Ohio and West Virginia, was acquired by Syracuse, New York-based Penn Traffic in 1989. As a result of Penn Traffic's 2003 bankruptcy, all stores were either closed or sold to other companies.

86. Dave

Born on July 2, 1932, in Atlantic City, New Jersey, David "Dave" Thomas was adopted by a Kalamazoo, Michigan, family at the age of six months. By the time he was fifteen, the family had moved to Fort Wayne, Indiana, where Dave dropped out of school in the 10th grade in order to work full-time at the local Hobby House restaurant.

Returning to Fort Wayne after serving in the Army during the Korean War, he found that his former boss had purchased some of the first franchises of the fledgling Kentucky Fried Chicken restaurant chain. He offered Dave the opportunity to run the unit in Columbus.

After complaining that he couldn't find a good hamburger in Columbus, Thomas decided to open his own fast food restaurant (see **Where's the Beef?** page 28). On November 15, 1969, he opened the first Wendy's, named for his eight-year-old daughter, Melinda Lou, known as Wendy, youngest of his five children with his wife Lorraine, whom he married in 1956. Known for its square hamburgers and choice of toppings, Wendy's quickly caught on and within less than a decade grew into a franchise of 1,000 stores.

Wearing a Wendy's apron, Thomas was one of the nation's most recognized television spokesmen, appearing in almost every advertisement for the chain. At the time of his death in 2002, there were more than 6,000 Wendy's restaurants operating in North America.

87. Playmates

Born in Columbus on February 8, 1971, Heidi Mark was discovered working at a local Hooters and appeared on the cover of the April 1994 issue of *Playboy Magazine* featuring "The Girls of Hooters." She was chosen as *Playboy's* Playmate of the Month in July 1995. Following her Playmate debut, Heidi became a Born-Again Christian, explaining that she frequently read a "little pink Bible" and believed angels helped her to overcome her fear of flying. She became an actress and has appeared in films including *Swimsuit: The Movie*, *Life Without Dick*, *Baywatch Hawaii*, *Weapons of Mass Distraction*, and *Man of the Year*. Heidi married Vince Neil, lead singer of Mötley Crüe, on May 28, 2000, at the Beverly Hills restaurant Le O'rangerie, then filed for divorce after 15 months, citing "irreconcilable differences."

Born in Norton, Ohio, on November 23, 1978, Sandra Hubby represented Columbus in the Miss Hawaiian Tropic Pageant, then later became *Playboy Magazine's* March 2004 Playmate of the Month. She appeared as the April girl in the 2005 *Playboy* swimsuit calendar, the inaugural "Playmates at Play" calendar, shot on the grounds of the Playboy Mansion. It was *Playboy's* first attempt at creating a non-nude swimsuit calendar featuring Playmates, similar in style to the *Sports Illustrated* swimsuit calendars.

88. Ellen Griswold

Born in Columbus on November 15, 1951, the daughter of Priscilla Smith, a violinist, and Gene D'Angelo, a bass player and television station manager, Beverly D'Angelo began work in the theatre, appearing on Broadway in 1976 in *Rockabye Hamlet* (also known as *Kronborg: 1582*) a musical based on Shakespeare's *Hamlet*. Although the production was a failure, running less than a month, D'Angelo's performance as Ophelia attracted positive attention.

After gaining minor roles in movies including *Annie Hall*, D'Angelo appeared in a string of hit movies in the late 1970s, appearing in *Every Which Way But Loose*, *Hair* and *Coal Miner's Daughter*. Her biggest break came with Chevy Chase in the 1983 *National Lampoon's Vacation*. Her role as Ellen Griswold was reprised in three *Vacation* sequels from 1985 through 1997.

In 1981, she married Italian aristocrat, Duke Lorenzo Salviati, a direct descendant of Lorenzo de Medici. After they separated in 1983, she became involved with Al Pacino. She had previously met him in 1988 when auditioning for the film, *Sea of Love*. They lived together from 1996 to 2003.

Beverly's maternal grandfather, Howard Dwight Smith, was the architect who designed Ohio Stadium also known as "the Horseshoe" (see **Monument to College Football**, page 35) at Ohio State.

89. "Black Edison"

Born in Columbus on April 23, 1856, Granville T. Woods, an African-American, attended local schools until age 10, when he then went to work with his father, repairing railroad equipment and machinery. He later found work operating a steam locomotive for the Danville and Southern Railroad. In 1884, he and his brother Lyates formed the Woods Railway Telegraph Company, manufacturer of telephone and telegraph equipment. A year later, he patented an apparatus which was a combination of a telephone and a telegraph. The device, which he called the "telegraphony," allowed a telegraph station to send voice and telegraph messages over a single wire. He sold the rights to this device to the American Bell Telephone Company.

In 1887, Woods patented the Synchronous Multiplex Railway Telegraph, which allowed moving trains to communicate with other trains and train stations, thus improving railway efficiency and safety. In 1888, he manufactured a system of overhead electric conducting lines for railroads modeled after the system pioneered by Charles van Depoele, a famed inventor who had by then installed his electric railway system in thirteen American cities.

By the time of his death in 1910, Woods had made a successful career as an engineer and inventor, and was referred to by some as the "Black Edison."

90. Oh Henry!

Over the years, the prison population at the Ohio Penitentiary (see **Pen Pals**, page 36) in Columbus included such characters as Confederate General John H. Morgan, Col. Basil W. Duke (President Jefferson Davis' bodyguard), Prohibition-era gangster George "Bugs" Moran, Dr. Sam Sheppard (whose story inspired *The Fugitive*), and William Sydney Porter, a teller at the First National Bank in Austin, Texas, who was convicted of embezzlement.

Prison gates slammed shut behind Porter on April 25, 1898. Alone in his cell, inmate No. 30664 wrote short stories, most notably, *The Gift of the Magi*, about a young married couple and how they deal with the challenge of buying secret Christmas gifts for each other with very little money. He sent manuscripts to a relative of a fellow prisoner who then forwarded them to a publisher. Porter did not sign his real name to any of his works, instead using "O. Henry," the pseudonym constructed from the first two letters of OHio and the second and last two of pENitentiaRY.

On July 21, 1901, exactly three years, two months and 27 days after he entered the penitentiary, Porter was discharged, moved to New York, and continued to write. His wit, characterization, and plot twists were adored by his readers. But Porter drank heavily and his health began to deteriorate. Twelve years after his discharge from prison, the world mourned the death of one of its favorite authors.

91. Rocky Road

One of the first major highways in the country to be built entirely by the federal government and the first American road to use macadam (compacted gravel) surfacing, the National Road (or Cumberland Road) reached the city in 1831, connecting Columbus to Baltimore and other cities along the east coast. The National Road opened the Ohio River Valley and the Midwest for settlement and commerce.

Funding for the National Road was authorized on March 29, 1806 by President Thomas Jefferson. Construction began in 1811 at Cumberland, Maryland, on the Potomac River. It crossed the Allegheny Mountains and southwestern Pennsylvania, reaching Wheeling, Virginia (now West Virginia) on the Ohio River in 1818. From 1825 to 1838, the road was extended across Ohio. At first, the two most common vehicles were the stagecoach and the Conestoga wagon. It is estimated there was about one tavern every mile on the National Road.

50% of the United States population lives within a 500 mile radius of Columbus. It has a driving distance of less than four hours from Cincinnati, Cleveland, Detroit, Fort Wayne, Indianapolis, Lexington, Louisville, Pittsburgh, and Toledo. Likewise, Chicago, Milwaukee, Nashville, New York City, Washington, DC, St Louis, Atlanta, Charlotte, and Philadelphia are all within a day's drive of the city.

92. Man in the Street

Born in Columbus on October 17, 1921, the son of Margaret and George Poston, a liquor salesman and dairy chemist, Thomas Gordon "Tom" Poston attended Bethany College in West Virginia, but did not graduate. Instead, he joined the Air Force in 1941. Accepted to officer candidate school and then graduating from flight training, Poston served as a pilot in the European theater in World War II; his aircraft dropped paratroopers for the Normandy invasion. He served in North Africa, Italy, France, and England. After his discharge, Poston began studying acting in New York City.

His run as a comic bumbler began in the mid-1950s on *The Steve Allen Show* after Allen plucked the character actor from the Broadway stage to join an ensemble of eccentrics for "Man in the Street" interviews. For these performances, Poston won the 1959 Emmy Award for "Best Supporting Actor in a Comedy Series." Don Knotts was the shaky Mr. Morrison, Louis Nye was the suave, overconfident Gordon Hathaway and Poston's character was so unnerved by the television cameras that he couldn't remember who he was.

Poston was a recurring guest star on *The Bob Newhart Show* in the 1970s. In 2001, he married actress Suzanne Pleshette, who played the wife of Newhart's character on the show.

93. Eye of the Beholder

She was the local hazel-eyed, auburn-haired beauty who, entered as "Miss Columbus," won the 1922 Miss America pageant. Mary Katherine Campbell (born in Columbus on December 18, 1905) had just received her diploma from East High School in February of that year. She enrolled at Ohio State as an Art Major immediately after her selection.

She was also only fifteen at the time, which was against pageant rules, however, she lied on her application so that she could compete. She competed the next year in 1923, once again representing Columbus, and won the title again, the only person to win the Miss America Pageant twice. As a result of her winning two and almost a third title in 1924, the rules were changed to allow a contestant to earn the title only once.

Joseph Cummings Chase, one of the judges said, "Miss Campbell is possessed of great vivacity and an inherent shyness that constitute a wonderful combination. She is typically American and altogether an ideal type. Her forebearers for ten generations have been American born."

Mary Katherine received offers to do three movies, two musical comedies, a circus, and vaudeville. She was even approached by Florenz Ziegfeld, "Glorifier of the American Girl," to join the famous "Follies," but her mother wouldn't hear of it. She married Frederick Townley, a DuPont executive, and lived a quiet life until her death in 1990.

94. Hondo

Born on April 8, 1940, in Martins Ferry, Ohio, John Havlicek was a three-sport standout athlete at Bridgeport High School. Focusing on basketball at Ohio State, he was named a collegiate All-American, averaging 14.6 points per game in three varsity seasons along with Buckeye teammates including Jerry Lucas, Mel Nowell, Larry Siegried, Joe Roberts, and Bobby Knight (see **The General**, page 69). His Ohio State teams compiled an impressive 78-6 record and captured the NCAA Championship in 1960.

Havlicek went on to play for the Boston Celtics, scoring 26,395 points (20.8 points per game, 11th all-time scorer in the NBA). Nicknamed "Hondo" (inspired by the John Wayne movie of the same name), Havlicek revolutionized the "sixth man" role, and has been immortalized for his clutch steal in the closing seconds of the 1965 Eastern Conference championship.

During his playing career, Havlicek spent his off-seasons in Columbus where he became a close friend of Dave Thomas (see **Dave**, page 86), the founder of Wendy's restaurants. Thomas's daughter, Wendy, whom the franchise is named after, worked as a babysitter for Havlicek's two children. Shortly after his playing career ended, Havlicek decided to buy his own Wendy's franchises, securing the rights to Westchester County outside of New York City.

95. Yours 'Til Hayden Falls

Just south of Hayden Run Road in northwest Columbus is a 25-foot waterfall, for many years one of the city's best-kept secrets. Hayden Run (originally called Roaring Run) is a small stream that enters a narrow, rocky gorge, and just before it winds its way down to the Scioto River, it tumbles over a ledge of limestone rock (see **Stone That Built Columbus**, page 30), forming a cascade known as Hayden Falls. The quantity and quality of this cataract depends heavily on the amount of rainfall – sometimes it's just a trickle, and other times it's a splendid falls.

Until recently, the area was a wild looking gorge, and despite its location in a residential area with houses lining its southern edge, it is not well-known even to locals. There is a parking lot on the south side of Hayden Run Road. From there if you walk towards the river, you'll find a trail going down into the gorge. This trail leads to the waterfalls. A stairway down into the gorge and a boardwalk near the base of the falls were added in 2005. (In high water, the boardwalk is inaccessible).

To reach Hayden Falls from I-270, take Exit 15 and head east on Tuttle Crossing Boulevard. Take a right onto Franz Road, then a left onto Hayden Run Road. The parking area is on the right.

96. House Calls in Columbus

Nathan and Lucy Goodale, along with their six-year-old son Lincoln, left Worchester, Massachusetts, in 1788, and settled in Marietta, Ohio. On March 1, 1793, Nathan was working his farm when he disappeared. Moccasin footprints in the snow revealed he had been captured by Indians. Left as the man of the family, young Lincoln decided to take up the study of medicine, training under Dr. Leonard Jewett of Athens County.

In 1805, Lincoln and his widowed mother came to Franklinton (see **The City That Almost Wasn't**, page 1), now part of the city of Columbus. He was 23 and the first physician to settle in the county. At that time, central Ohio was still a wild and unsettled place. Early settlers lived in fear of Indian attacks, and as late as 1811 there was not yet a church, schoolhouse, or bridge over any stream within 100 miles. To reach his patients he would cross streams on horseback or hike through dark forests in the middle of the night.

Lincoln Goodale was also a successful businessman whose wealth and generosity allowed him to provide free medical care to the poor. He was a great benefactor to the city and his legacy includes a large parcel of land that today is known as Goodale Park. He offered the acreage to the Columbus City Council on Bastille Day, French liberation day, July 14, 1851. His likeness in the form of a large bronze statue watches over the park.

97. Pop Art

Born in Manhattan into an upper-middle-class New York City family, Roy Lichtenstein attended the Franklin School for Boys, then left New York to study fine arts at Ohio State. A three year stint in the army during World War II interrupted his studies before he returned to OSU under the supervision of Hoyt L. Sherman. Professor Sherman employed the "flash room," a darkened room where images would be briefly flashed onto the screen. His students were supposed to draw what they had seen. This method of grasping an image by copying it would later be cited by Lichtenstein as having had an influence on his work.

In 1961, Lichtenstein began his first "Pop Art" paintings using thick outlines, bold colors, and Ben-day Dots to represent certain colors, as if created by photographic reproduction. His signature style borrowed from mass culture – particularly comic books and advertising – bringing the look and feel of commercial printing to fine art. His first work to feature the large-scale use of hard-edged figures and small colored dots was "Look Mickey." In the same year he produced six other works with recognizable characters from gum wrappers and cartoons.

Next to Andy Warhol, Roy Lichtenstein is considered as the great artist of the Pop Art movement.

98. First Day of Kindergarten

A German school teacher by the name of Friedrich Froebel believed that a child's growth resembled that of a plant in a garden. He put his concept into practice in an institution for preschool children in Blankenburg in 1837. The German word "kindergarten" (child's garden) was formally applied to it in 1840.

Caroline Louisa Frankenberg studied with Froebel while his educational theories were still developing and evolving. She traveled to America to join relatives in Columbus in 1836, eager to spread his ideas in a new country. Once settled here, she started a small school in the city's German Village (see **Die Nachbarschaft**, page 63). But despite her dreams and dedication, the school did not succeed, and she returned to Germany

Strengthened by additional years with Froebel, Miss Frankenberg returned to Columbus in 1858 to establish a school, this time with all the elements of her mentor's kindergarten program. Her classroom was a cheerful place where children sang and played. They were busy with occupations such as paper folding and clay modeling. It was a unique new concept and the first program of its kind in America.

In 1859, while teaching at an infant school in Concord, Massachusetts, Elizabeth Palmer Peabody heard of Frankenberg's school, and a year after visiting her in Columbus, Peabody opened a kindergarten in Boston, the first English-speaking one of its kind in the United States.

99. Thanksgiving Shuffle

For 75 years after Abraham Lincoln issued the first Thanksgiving Proclamation, succeeding Presidents continued to honor the tradition, declaring the last Thursday in November as the day of Thanksgiving. However, in 1939, the last Thursday of November was going to fall on November 30th, leaving only 24 shopping days until Christmas.

In 1939, the American economy had yet to fully recover from the Great Depression. Without informing his family, Fred Lazarus, Jr. of F&R Lazarus & Company (see **Raising Lazarus**, page 12) asked President Franklin Roosevelt to move Thanksgiving Day a week earlier in order to increase the shopping days before Christmas, hoping that with an extra week of shopping, people would buy more. Roosevelt liked the idea and declared Thanksgiving to be Thursday, November 23, the second-to-last Thursday of the month.

On hearing the President's decision, Fred's brother Simon was upset since the new date disrupted the scheduled OSU Thanksgiving football game. "What damn fool got the President to do that?" he demanded. "You're looking at him," said Fred.

On December 26, 1941, Congress passed a law declaring that Thanksgiving would occur every year on the fourth Thursday of November, ensuring a stable timetable for the official beginning of the Christmas shopping season.

100. Making an Impression

French artist Georges Seurat spent two years painting "A Sunday afternoon on the Island of LaGrande Jatte," one of the most revered works of the neo-impressionist movement during the late 19th century. The ten-foot-wide canvas, depicting the public park on the island in the Seine, is now in the permanent collection of the Art Institute of Chicago.

A local sculptor, James T. Mason began working for the Columbus Recreation and Parks Department in 1978, teaching at the Cultural Arts Center. In 1988, he created the sculptural frames that began to coax yew trees into shapes, and over the next four years he installed a re-creation of Seurat's painting in sculpted shrubbery (topiary) on the 10-acre site of what was once the Ohio School for the Deaf. It is the only topiary interpretation of a painting in existence. This landscape of "a painting of a landscape" includes 54 people, eight boats with sails of clematis, three dogs, a monkey and a cat. The largest topiary is 12 feet tall. Elaine Mason, a retired arts coordinator for the Department, trained city gardeners to trim the figures.

A pond, representing the River Seine, was installed in 1989, along with the hills. Seurat would have sketched his scene from the top of the easterly hill. If you stand left of the bronze plaque on the stone slab in the path, you will see "the painting" as the artist saw it.

101. Not the Only One

Although our own Columbus is the largest by far, no fewer than sixteen other states have cities named for the 15th century Italian explorer, including Arkansas, Georgia, Illinois, Indiana, Kansas, Kentucky, Mississippi, Montana, Nebraska, New Jersey, New Mexico, New York, North Carolina, North Dakota, Texas, and Wisconsin (site of the Christopher Columbus Museum). States with a "Columbus Township" include Illinois, Indiana, Iowa, Michigan, Michigan, Minnesota, Missouri, Nebraska, North Carolina, and Pennsylvania. There is a "Columbus City" in Iowa, a "Columbus Junction" in Iowa, and a "Columbus Grove" in Putnam County, right here in our own state of Ohio.

The first city, as well as the first-planned capital, in America named for Christopher Columbus was founded March 26, 1786, as the center of government, education, and commerce in South Carolina. Columbus, Ohio (see **The City That Almost Wasn't**, page 1), was laid out and named 26 years later.

Within city limits, Columbus has more people than Boston, Denver, Atlanta, Miami, or Seattle, and more than its Ohio cousins Cincinnati and Cleveland, according to U.S. Census figures.

"Adapt yourselves to the things among which your lot has been cast and love sincerely the fellow creatures with whom destiny has ordained that you shall live."

— Marcus Aurelius

Even if you live in Columbus .

About the Author

Horace Martin Woodhouse is a celebrated traveler, intrepid explorer, professor of cultural archaeology, and dedicated vagabond. As an author he is both a romantic and a cynic whose writings have appeared in books, anthologies, magazines, newspapers, professional journals, and on the Internet. Over the course of his many years of travel, education, adventure and misadventure, Woodhouse has cultivated an intense curiosity about the most interesting people and places in America.

About Curiosity Company

A book publisher without many of the overheads associated with traditional methods, Curiosity Company is prepared to take risks that would probably have other publishers waking up in a cold sweat in the middle of the night. Our goal is to publish works we like, works we believe in, which should be the only reason for anybody to publish anything. Each Curiosity Company book is intended to grab you by the throat, demanding to be read or to pick away at the back of your brain until there is no choice but to go for it. Are you more curious about us? Go to: www.curiositycompany.com

NOTES

NOTES

NOTES

Made in the USA
Monee, IL
21 January 2020